CRITICAL CONDITION

The Danger of Being Overly Critical and Judgmental

James A. McMenis

PRESS

Critical Condition
The Danger of Being Overly Critical and Judgmental
by James A. Mcmenis

Printed in the United States of America.

ISBN 9781498473064

Unless otherwise indicated, Scripture quotations taken from the King James Version (KJV) – *public domain.*

www.xulonpress.com

Table of Contents

Chapter 1

INTRODUCTION

---❖---

I accepted Jesus Christ as my Savior at the age of seventeen. Immediately after this decision, I had a desire to know His Word, fellowship with other believers, and become involved in the church. I remember receiving the gift of a brand new Bible after my baptism. I knew with everything in me that my life had changed. I can remember the enthusiasm of wanting others to know this same Jesus who had saved me and given me a new perspective on life—and eternity. I had a deep desire to learn His Word and to share it with others. From that moment, I have never been the same! If I were to be real with you about my life, walk of faith, and call as a minister, there's one thing that the enemy has used more than anything else to derail me—criticism. Through the years, I have found myself—spiritually and mentally speaking—in *critical condition*. Whether I was being met by the criticism of those in the religious community or allowing a critical mindset into my own life, I have discovered that a critical spirit is dangerous.

So why write a book on being critical? Wouldn't it seem critical to write a book about the danger of being critical? Ha-ha! I have pondered these questions and challenged myself with them. However, I strongly feel that criticism is negatively affecting our marriages, homes, churches, communities and, above all, the work of the Gospel.

I had a rude awakening to criticism shortly after entering the ministry. I was invited to speak at a close friend's family church; it was a small church outside of Shreveport, and it was my first speaking engagement. I was eighteen years old and excited to have the opportunity to speak at a Sunday "Youth Day" service. This decision was met with criticism. An individual that was dear to me criticized me for speaking at a "black" church. I cannot express to you how heartbreaking this was for me. I did not let it sway me, but it did trouble me to a great degree. How could someone be criticized for preaching the Word of God to anyone? I didn't understand it at all! I was raised to believe the truth that all men were created in the image of God, and that He is no respecter of persons. The criticism I faced was not based on anything biblical. It had no righteous merit. Why, then, was I criticized? Why does anyone criticize another? What is the root of criticism? Within the following chapters, I hope to dissect these questions and find the answers we need in God's Word.

Shortly after my call into the ministry, I found myself filling the pulpit at my church while our leaders sought to find a pastor, as my pastor had resigned shortly after I was saved. The associate pastor also resigned, and I witnessed the church suffer a heart-wrenching split as an initiation to my walk of faith. It is only by God's grace and sovereign plan for my life that I endured and remained in church after witnessing these things. One of our deacons (the only deacon that faithfully attended) asked me to teach Sunday school. He also wanted me to preach on Sundays and Wednesdays until they found a pastor. I had not been saved for long, but I had a passion for God's Word, so I welcomed and accepted the call. I remember being met immediately with criticism. I was told that I used too many Scriptures in my messages. I was asked to start using only one or two references as a "text" to my sermon. I remember thinking of how that went against the conviction I had from God's Spirit. I had a desire to know His Word and to share it. Yet, I was being told that my method was not right—and it did not end there. Actively serving in ministry opened my eyes to a side of church life that I would have never known existed—a world of criticism. I am not saying it was all bad, nor am I saying that every church is filled with critics. I am simply sharing what I was experiencing at the time.

One day while our worship leader was conducting the worship service, an older (charter) member attended the service. She quickly noticed that we were singing out of the newer hymn books. No one knew that her family, many years before, had purchased the older hymn books. She immediately went into the storage room and began to pass out the older hymn books. She walked up to the worship leader and gave him the older version as well. I know you are wondering what he did. He turned to the next hymn in the book she gave him while announcing the hymn number. I could not believe my eyes! This woman, whom I had rarely seen, walked in and took over the worship service all because she did not like the newer hymn books! The new book had all the songs the older ones had. Why would she do such a thing? Why was it allowed? How did that affect others who had come to worship that day?

"Brother James, you'll need to shave that facial hair if you're gonna serve here." I remember being struck by those words at the age of 18. I had no problem shaving my little mustache. My cousin's advice was to put some milk on it and let the cat lick it off. My problem was not shaving; it was that I had read that Jesus had a beard. Why be critical? This was only the beginning of the many criticisms that I would soon hear. I am sure you have heard similar ones as well.

"You'll need to go buy some clothes for church." "I can't believe she wore pants to church." "That preacher went a little too long today." "I wish he'd use another text besides the Book of Romans." "Can you believe so and so was at church after what I heard they were doing last week?" "Did

I see you talking to that heathen? Don't you know that they are not saved? I hope you were only telling them they need to get right with God!" "That music is too loud!" "The sanctuary is too cold." "Can you believe she cut her hair that short?" "I heard they were going to miss the evening service for a football game." "That preacher talks about giving too much." "Have you seen her husband? Surely they can afford better clothes than that." "I can't believe that man came to church with such an awful smell." "Did you know that couple didn't even bring a dish to the pot-luck dinner? And did you see how much they put on their plate?" "I can't believe that family sat on that pew. Don't they know that's where the Smiths sit?"

These are but a fraction of the criticisms I heard early in my walk of faith. They have not stopped; in fact, they keep coming. Today, through social media, the voice of the critic is louder than ever. It seems today that everyone has a voice and many use their platforms only to criticize others. This negative, hard, and critical spirit leaves a wake of brokenness, depression and sadly, even suicide. I believe that our world is in "Critical Condition." As believers, we must break the hold of this self-righteous and condemning attitude.

Consider how criticism plagues society. How many lives have been devastated by bullies who constantly bombard their prey with unmerited criticism? Height, size, shape, skin tone, color, class, social status, ethnicity, style, and even autism are all used as the basis for demeaning criticism. Criticism is without a doubt a major contributing factor to the mental health and stability of our young people.

Suicide is the SECOND leading cause of death for ages 10-24. (2013 CDC WISQARS). Suicide is the SECOND leading cause of death for college-age youth and ages 12-18. (2013 CDC WISQARS). More teenagers and young adults die from suicide than from cancer, heart disease, AIDS, birth defects, stroke, pneumonia, influenza, and chronic lung disease, COMBINED. Each day in our nation there are an average of over 5,400 attempts by young people grades 7-12. [http://jasonfoundation. com/prp/facts/youth-suicide-statistics]

These statistics are alarming. I only share them with you to awaken you to the reality of the world we are living in and its need for grace, love and acceptance that can only come through the Gospel of Jesus Christ. Today's culture has a voice that is unprecedented. The avenues of smart phones and social media have created a climate that is unlike anything our parents or grandparents ever experienced. The quiet criticism of a private conversation can now reach thousands with the simple touch of a screen—*retweet, like, send, post.*

Our news outlets are constantly flooding our television screens with reports of protests, riots, and rallies that are centered on hate. We live in a world that thinks the answer to violence is more violence and that hate can overcome hate. People are being polarized, separated, and divided by a spirit of prejudice and hate. I am reminded of the words of Dr. Martin Luther King:

Darkness cannot drive out darkness;
only light can do that.
Hate cannot drive out hate;
only love can do that.
Hate multiplies hate,
violence multiplies violence,
and toughness multiplies toughness

in a descending spiral of destruction....
The chain reaction of evil —
hate begetting hate,
wars producing more wars —
must be broken,
or we shall be plunged
into the dark abyss of annihilation.

[Dr. Martin Luther King, Jr., *Strength To Love*, 1963]

What causes people to be so polarized? Why do we allow ourselves to become so critical of others? What are the grounds for our constant judgments and condemning mindsets? Whether it is political, social, or religious in nature, I believe we have all been affected by the power of negative and demeaning criticism.

Chapter 2

THE "CRITICAL" CONDITION

A critical spirit is dangerous. It is vital to understand the spirit of criticism, how it operates, and the fruit it produces. It wreaks havoc in marriages, relationships and will suck the joy right out of your life. The spirit of criticism is not of God. Satan loves to cause division and he knows that a critical spirit will keep believers from reaching their full potential in Christ. In this book, we will look at some of the root causes of criticism. I truly desire to get to the root of criticism. I pray that you will learn how to recognize and deal with a critical spirit using the Word of God. In doing so, you can avoid falling into the trap that is plaguing our homes, churches and society and truly leaving many in critical condition.

To criticize means to act as a critic, to consider the merits and demerits of someone or something. It is to blame, condemn, denounce, dis, knock, come down on, or find fault with another. When we criticize, we are taking on a position of judgment that God has not given us the right to fulfill. The Word of God makes this clear. Consider what Paul said to the Corinthians:

> *But with me it is a very small thing that I should be judged*
> *of you, or of man's judgment: yea, I judge not mine own self.*

*For I know nothing by myself; yet am I not hereby justified:
but he that judgeth me is the Lord. Therefore judge nothing
before the time, until the Lord come, who both will bring to
light the hidden things of darkness, and will make manifest
the counsels of the hearts: and then shall every man have
praise of God* (1 Corinthians 4:3-5).

There can be no criticism without judgment being involved. The Lord's
mandate through the Apostle Paul was absolutely clear. We are not to
judge another. God is judge, and we must trust Him to judge righteously.
Jesus spoke about judgment as He preached the Sermon on the Mount.

*And why beholdest thou the mote that is in thy brother's eye,
but perceivest not the beam that is in thine own eye? Either
how canst thou say to thy brother, Brother, let me pull out
the mote that is in thine eye, when thou thyself beholdest
not the beam that is in thine own eye? Thou hypocrite, cast
out first the beam out of thine own eye, and then shalt thou
see clearly to pull out the mote that is in thy brother's eye*
(Luke 6:41-42).

He was speaking in the context of relationships, judgment and mercy.
We all get tempted to be critical of others, but Jesus called it hypocritical.
Criticism divides. It has the power to destroy marriages, ruin relationships
and hinder the work of the Gospel. As believers, we have to be careful not
to allow a critical spirit to take root in our lives and churches. Instead, we
would be wise to take Jesus' advice and consider what may need correcting
in ourselves. After all, we will reap what we sow.

Be ye therefore merciful, as your Father also is merciful. Judge not, and ye shall not be judged: condemn not, and ye shall not be condemned: forgive, and ye shall be forgiven: Give, and it shall be given unto you; good measure, pressed down, and shaken together, and running over, shall men give into your bosom. For with the same measure that ye mete withal it shall be measured to you again (Luke 6:36-38).

The same is recorded in the Gospel of Matthew:

Judge not, that ye be not judged. For with what judgment ye judge, ye shall be judged: and with what measure ye mete, it shall be measured to you again. And why beholdest thou the mote that is in thy brother's eye, but considerest not the beam that is in thine own eye? Or how wilt thou say to thy brother, Let me pull out the mote out of thine eye; and, behold, a beam is in thine own eye? Thou hypocrite, first cast out the beam out of thine own eye; and then shalt thou see clearly to cast out the mote out of thy brother's eye (Matthew 7:1-5).

Again, this is reiterated in the New Testament:

But why dost thou judge thy brother? or why dost thou set at nought thy brother? For we shall all stand before the judgment seat of Christ (Romans 14:10).

SOUND JUDGMENT

Before I proceed, let me be clear in the type of criticism we are dealing with in this book. There is a difference between making sound judgment calls and being critically judgmental. We are certainly expected to have sound judgment in the decisions we make as it relates to the well-being of our lives and families. For example, we must use good judgment in who we will allow to babysit our kids. It is wise to use sound judgment when choosing a spouse. We are called to make judgments in who we allow to speak into our lives, influence us and lead our society. These types of judgments are needful because they are about building a solid life by making wise decisions based on the Word of God. However, they are entirely different than the type of judgment we're going to discuss. The purpose of this book is to address the dangers of being judgmental in a critical way as it relates to others.

ARE YOU CRITICAL?

For if we would judge ourselves, we should not be judged (1 Corinthians 11:31).

Ask yourself what you are giving, because that is what you will get back from others. Are you giving forgiveness? Judgment? Mercy? Do not sow what you do not wish to reap. Relationships are a foundational part of life. In fact, the quality of your life will never go beyond the quality of your relationships. God expects us to be good stewards over the relationships He has put in our lives. As Christians, it is vital that we be cordial and relational as a means to invite others into the same saving grace that we have come to know.

It is likely that we have all experienced times in a relationship where we are more critical than others. It is easy to overlook the faults of our spouse after a wonderful romantic night together. It is in the moments where things aren't so easy that we become hyper-aware of others' shortcomings and we are most tempted to criticize and even condemn.

You may be thinking, "What if I have a good and justified reason?" Sometimes there is a legitimate reason to find fault, but that does not mean you should. When criticism feels justified it is important to remember Jesus' words from the Sermon on the Mount, *"Be ye merciful, as your Father also is merciful"* (Luke 6:36). You may think you have all the reason in the world to criticize. To paraphrase Matthew 7:1-5, Jesus said it is better to make sure you get that telephone pole out of your eye before you try to get the toothpick out of your spouse's eye. When forgiveness becomes difficult, think about all that the Lord has forgiven you. Whatever it is that you feel your spouse, friend, or relative has done wrong, Jesus sees it. No one is perfect. We all make mistakes. There is only one perfect, and that is Jesus Christ. The same grace you extend to another may be the same grace you will need from them one day.

I truly believe that the *critical condition* mindset can distort the way we see others. Are you guilty of judging others for the sin of your own heart? A friend of mine recently shared with me a message he had heard from Dr. Ravi Zacharias.

> I heard a cute little story, growing up in India. It is the story of a little boy who had lots of pretty marbles. But he was constantly eyeing his sister's bagful of candy. One day he said to her, "If you give me all your candy, I'll give you all of my marbles." She gave it much thought, and agreed to the trade. He took all her candy and went back

to his room to get his marbles. But the more he admired them the more reluctant he became to give them all up. So he hid the best of them under his pillow and took the rest to her. That night, she slept soundly, while he tossed and turned restlessly, unable to sleep and thinking, "I wonder if she gave me all the candy?" [Ravi Zacharias, "Embodied Truth"]

How is it that we can focus on the perceived wrongdoing of others while overlooking our own sin? We must remember to judge ourselves first. None of us are without sin. Think of the audacity it requires to focus on the wrong of another while overlooking the wrong you have done. In the story above, judgment was clouded by perceived guilt. Are you allowing your own sin to distort the way you see others?

A BETTER WAY

For as the heavens are higher than the earth, so are my ways higher than your ways, and my thoughts than your thoughts (Isaiah 55:9).

There is a better way to handle these critical comments and situations that will bring God glory. Instead of pointing out the bad in the one who has offended you, find something good about them, and focus your thoughts there. Find something that offers potential and hope. Speak life into that person, especially when they have wronged you; it is a decisive act that truly reflects Jesus in the earth. It mirrors the forgiving and sacrificial love He has already given to us. We are called to live as Christ and to demonstrate His love that is sacrificial in nature.

*But God commendeth His love towards us, in that, while we
were yet sinners, Christ died for the ungodly* (Romans 5:8).

Take a moment to think this over. This verse applies to everyone. We were all born into sin and all are guilty according to God's law. We were doing nothing to pursue Him, yet He pursued us. He could have said, "They didn't obey me. They deserve the punishment they're going to get." Thankfully, that was not God's heart at all. He chose, in the midst of our ungodliness, to have grace and mercy. It is easy to forget where we would be if God had not made a way to salvation. Even when we were *"enemies,"* He reconciled us through the death of His Son (Romans 5:10). Even though we deserved punishment, and God would have been justified in giving it to us, He instead chose to give us the most valuable gift He had, His son Jesus. It makes our problems seem quite small when viewed in the light of all that Jesus Christ has done for us. The least we can do is give mercy as we have been given mercy—even if we feel someone does not deserve it.

*Herein is love, not that we loved God, but that He loved us,
and sent His Son to be the propitiation for our sins. Beloved,
if God so loved us, we ought also to love one another* (1
John 4:10-11).

You may be in a difficult situation. Do not quench the work of the Holy Spirit by persisting to act as a critic. You cannot change anyone but yourself. Trying to change others is a fruitless endeavor. Only God can do that. Instead of trying forcibly to change your spouse, pray for them. Start praying and asking the Lord, "What can I change about myself?"

Every single marriage and relationship has the potential to see God glorified if we will step out of the spirit of criticism. The next time you feel the need to criticize, stop to think, pray and seek God. Judge yourself before you go and criticize your spouse, friend, and co-worker. If God unconditionally loves us, we should unconditionally love others. That means we love, even when our conditions are not met.

LOVE COVERS

And above all things have fervent charity [love] among yourselves: for charity [love] shall cover the multitude of sins (1 Peter 4:8).

God said to fervently love. This is an intensely intentional decision on our part to let love be bigger than the shortcomings of others. Fervent love can be applied in so many ways. We all know how difficult it can be to relent in the heat of an argument, when emotions are high. It is not easy because it does not appeal to our carnal and selfish nature. We want to hold our ground and prove our point. This is why God gave us His Holy Spirit. He knew we would need to lean on Him for supernatural power. He enables us to walk above our carnal nature and in a divine nature. Rest assured He will give you the strength you need.

According as his divine power hath given unto us all things that pertain unto life and godliness, through the knowledge of him that hath called us to glory and virtue: Whereby are given unto us exceeding great and precious promises: that by these ye might be partakers of the divine nature, having escaped the corruption that is in the world through lust. And beside this, giving all diligence, add to your faith virtue; and to virtue knowledge; And to knowledge temperance; and to temperance patience; and to patience godliness; And to godliness brotherly kindness; and to brotherly kindness charity. For if these things be in you, and abound, they make you that ye shall neither be barren nor unfruitful in the knowledge of our Lord Jesus Christ (2 Peter 1:3-8).

Imagine that you overheard a co-worker talking about you on the job. Your feelings are hurt. Your first instinct may be to go and talk about them behind their back, but fervent love covers. Instead of repaying evil for evil, God commands us to give the same mercy we have received. Maybe you don't agree with the way a family member is raising their kids or the way they spend their money. Instead of gossiping about them, show them the love of God. When we fervently and unconditionally love others, we are respecting God's divine order in which He is judge and we are ambassadors of His mercy.

Speak not evil one of another, brethren. He that speaketh evil of his brother, and judgeth his brother, speaketh evil of the law, and judgeth the law: but if thou judge the law, thou art not a doer of the law, but a judge (James 4:11).

Part of having an intimate relationship with God means that we know He is righteous. It means we have to trust that He will judge righteously. It means that we believe if there is a wrong, that He will make it right. When we refuse to step out of criticism, it is sort of like telling God that we think we can do His job better. Imagine telling God, "I don't trust you to handle this so I'm going to do it myself." This verse instructs us not to be a judge of the law but a doer. Thankfully, we do not need to act as judge. The Word tells us that God is righteous, and only He can judge.

> *God is the judge: He putteth down one, and setteth up another* (Psalms 75:7).

> *The heavens shall declare His righteousness: for God is judge Himself* (Psalm 50:6).

> *For the LORD is our judge, the LORD is our lawgiver, the LORD is our king; he will save us* (Isaiah 33:22).

> *Henceforth there is laid up for me a crown of righteousness, which the Lord, the righteous judge, shall give me at that day: and not me only, but unto all them also that love His appearing* (2 Timothy 4:8).

> *There is one lawgiver, who is able to save and to destroy; who art thou that judgest another?* (James 4:12).

When we are unconditionally good to others, especially when they have wronged us, we make a way for God to work in the situation. We are allowing Him to work on that person's heart and convict them as He sees fit. Isaiah tells us that His ways are not always our ways; they are higher. We may not understand them completely, but we can trust that they will work for the good. It is the only way to have joy in the situation.

> *For my thoughts are not your thoughts, neither are your ways my ways, saith the Lord. For as the heavens are higher*

than the earth, so are my ways higher than your ways, and
my thoughts than your thoughts. For as the rain cometh
down, and the snow from heaven, and returneth not thither,
but watereth the earth, and maketh it bring forth and bud,
that it may give seed to the sower, and bread to the eater: So
shall my word be that goeth forth out of my mouth: it shall
not return unto me void, but it shall accomplish that which
I please, and it shall prosper in the thing whereto I sent it.
For ye shall go out with joy, and be led forth with peace: the
mountains and the hills shall break forth before you into
singing, and all the trees of the field shall clap their hands
(Isaiah 55:8-12).

God's Word is clear; it is not our place to live as a critic. God is the only one who has the authority to judge. If we want God to work in our situation, we have to trust and honor Him.

In order to avoid the critical condition, we need to understand how it starts. Earlier we looked at Romans 14 where the question was asked, *"why dost thou judge thy brother?"* (v.10). It is a good question. What is it in us that finds it necessary to engage in how our neighbor mows their yard, or how they style their hair? Why do we find it necessary to criticize at all? Why must we focus in on every little thing that displeases us about our spouse? Why do we walk away from a powerful service, only to reflect on the message being too long or the temperature too low? Why must we look around the sanctuary and criticize others? Let's take a deeper look.

HYPOCRITICAL

Therefore thou art inexcusable, O man, whosoever thou art that judgest: for wherein thou judgest another, thou condemnest thyself; for thou that judgest doest the same things (Romans 2:1).

As a Christian, it saddens me to say this; but I believe some of the most critical people name the Name of Christ. This critical mindset does not represent the Savior of the world! The tag of 'hypocrite' is placed on people of faith more than any other group of people. *Hypo* means *under*. To be *hypo*-critical means that one lives beneath one's own criticism. In other words, when you judge someone, yet you do not live up to the standard by which you are judging others, you are a hypocrite. According to Romans 2:1, when we judge others, and are guilty as well, we condemn ourselves. The thing is you have to be *critical* in order to be called *hypo*critical.

Interestingly enough, Jesus used the word 'hypocrite' to describe the criticism of the self-righteous and religious (See Matthew 7:5, Luke 6:42, 13:15). *"An hypocrite with his mouth destroyeth his neighbour"* (Proverbs 11:9). Being hypocritical is a dangerous thing—it is destructive! There are many in the faith who cannot condemn enough. It is as though they wait for the opportunity to cast their judgments, criticize and condemn. If we are to see revival and the lost saved, we must break this spirit of self-righteousness. I have seen preachers condemned because of their clothing. Yet Jesus described the hypocrisy of judging John the Baptist for his clothing (See Matthew 11:7-10). I was once approached by someone who wanted to criticize the message of a guest pastor who had recently spoken to the church. The complaint was that the word "sin" was not used in his sermon.

24

Yet at the end of his message, over 120 souls accepted Christ! The truth is that the word "sin" was used many times (I personally heard the message). The point I am making is there are some so critical that they only see what they want to see and hear what they want to hear. I have been lambasted for everything you can imagine. I do not hear of these things from the world (the lost); it is church-going folk who are constantly dishing out their judgments.

I heard a well-known pastor once say, "I am not going to allow my critics to share the platform that God has given me to minister His Word, truth, love and grace." Therefore, he refused to use his platform to respond to criticism. I have adopted the same conviction in ministry. There is a dying world out there. Souls are lost, hurting, and broken. We should all be investing our energy to reach the lost—not for seeing how fast we can jump on social-media forums like Facebook and attack a preacher or sermon we did not like. I am convinced the lost world sees this behavior and uses it for justification for not seeking or honoring God. I had a man tell me that the reason he would never go to church was because all that he witnessed growing up were his religious relatives fighting about who was right in their interpretations. Thankfully, he is now saved and I am blessed to see him as a faithful member of our congregation. I believe many can hear his story and relate to it. We must break this negative cycle of *hypocrisy*.

Someone once told me that I didn't look like a preacher. To this, I responded, "I don't know what one looks like." My response was, "I don't know what one looks like." Since when are we supposed to be identified by suits, vests, and neckties? I had a woman ridicule me for not wearing a suit. She claimed I was trying to hide and live under-cover. To her, I did not dress like a pastor. Yet, this all happened in line at the nursery depart-ment of a home improvement store. I could not get over it. Am I supposed to wear a suit when buying plants for my flower beds—all because I am a "pastor"?

The number one reason people list as to why they don't attend church is, "I don't have anything to wear." Isn't that sad? Jesus was crucified naked while some church-folk judge others for their apparel! No one should be hesitant to receive God's Word, power and Spirit in the fellowship and assembly of believers because they are afraid that they will be judged by their clothing. I am not saying there isn't a proper attire or that we shouldn't dress modestly. The point I am making is that there is a lost world out there that needs Jesus; and sadly, hypocritical believers who love to point their fingers in criticism and judgment have misrepresented Him.

Before you think yourself high enough to judge and condemn others, search your own life. Jesus taught that if we would judge ourselves, we would not be judged (Matthew 7:1). May God raise up churches who are not known as "hypocrites." You may be wondering how that might be possible. Again, it is impossible to be *hypo*critical when you were never critical in the first place. When we choose to walk in love instead of judgment, we allow room for the Word of God and the work of the Holy Spirit to draw, convict, change and empower lives. Not only do we need to break this stigma, we need to learn how to respond to those who are overly critical.

On one occasion, my son and I were seated in a restaurant eating. In the booth right behind ours, I began to hear this man complaining about a church that he had recently visited. He was bothered by how long it took to baptize 38 people. He went on and on in negative criticism. It hit me that he was referring to our church. I could not get over his negativity. Worse, I was concerned for my young son who was hearing the same remarks as I was. I was concerned about how it would affect him. Why would a believer complain about such a thing (assuming he was a believer)? In my heart, I prayed and asked the Lord how to respond. He laid it on my heart to call the waitress and ask for their ticket. I paid their check, briefly spoke kindly to them and left. I can only hope that my response to their criticism paved the way for a change of heart towards the work of the Gospel. I needed my son to learn a valuable lesson. There will always be critics. No matter what you do, someone will find fault. I needed him to see how the Lord has called us to respond.

It hit me later that the critical conversation I was over-hearing likely had nothing to do with the time it took to baptize. I have found in many cases that criticism finds its root in other things, despite how it surfaces. It is my hope and prayer that we find the root to negative and destructive criticism and yank it out of our lives forever!

PRIDE: THE ROOT TO CRITICISM

PRIDE, n.–*Inordinate self-esteem; an unreasonable conceit of one's own superiority in talents, beauty, wealth, accomplishments, rank or elevation in office, which manifests itself in lofty airs, distance, reserve, and in contempt of others* (1828 Webster's Dictionary).

Criticism is not in harmony with the working of God's Spirit. Because of this, we must understand how to avoid it. In the following chapters, we are going to look at five things that can lead to a critical spirit. They can be summed up in one word, pride. In the following chapters, I will use the acrostic of PRIDE to study this list.

Preference
Resentment
Inferiority
Defensiveness
Envy

Chapter 3

PREFERENCE

M erriam-Webster defines *preference* as the feeling of liking or wanting one person or thing more than another, or an advantage that is given to some people or things and not others.

Our preference is a reflection of our personality. Having a preference is not a bad thing, but it must be kept in proper perspective. If we are not careful, a difference of opinion can lead to a conflict of preference, causing us to become critical of those who do not share our opinion or *preference*. Don't let your preference cause you to become a critic.

Let us say someone is hired in the office where you work. They have a bubbly personality and are outgoing. On the other hand, you are more of the quiet and reserved type. You find that you cannot handle the new personality that has come into the office. Maybe it exposes something about you that you are not happy about and it makes you uncomfortable. Maybe you wish you were more that way, and now it is in your face all the time. This is a personality conflict. Suddenly, you do not like the way this person dresses, you do not like the way they work... you even find yourself not liking anything about them. You may begin to accuse them of being flirtatious or cast them in a negative light. It is not because of anything that they ever did to you personally. It is your personal preference that has lead you to become critical and cast judgments.

Differences of opinion are inevitable because God created everyone with unique personalities. We are all made in His image. We may disagree, but that does not mean we have the right to criticize. The Bible gives great instruction on how we should react when we find ourselves in a conflict of preference:

> *Let love be without dissimulation. Abhor that which is evil; cleave to that which is good. Be kindly affectioned one to another with brotherly love; in honour preferring one another; not slothful in business; fervent in spirit; serving the Lord; rejoicing in hope; patient in tribulation; continuing instant in prayer; distributing to the necessity of the saints; given to hospitality. Bless them which persecute you: bless, and curse not... If it be possible, as much as it lieth in you, live peaceably with all men* (Romans 12:9-14, 18).

As children of God, we should take on the likeness of Jesus and love each other with a pure heart. This Scripture tells us to let our love be without dissimulation. In other words, do not let your love be 'two-faced'. *Dissimulate* means to hide under a false appearance. Have you ever met someone who treated you sweet and kind to your face, but then turned around and talked about you behind your back? That is dissimulated 'love' and we are to refrain from it. If someone treats us that way, we should show him or her genuine love in return. We will talk more about love later. True 'agape' love has everything to do with the loved and not the lover. It is sacrificial and does not require that any conditions be met. The world we live in is absorbed in an 'eros' love that has more to do with the lover than the loved. It is a selfish love that says, "I'll love you if you make me feel good; if you meet my conditions." Sadly, this type of love can generate criticism and division due to its selfish nature. Thank God that His love for us is true and pure—a love that is sacrificial.

I once heard Dr. Henry Cloud make an excellent point relating to this. During the 2016 Marriage Conference, he gave a great illustration about how we view our spouse in marriage. It is applicable to any relationship. To paraphrase his point, in marriage, there are only two seats we can sit in: the seat of judgment or the seat of mercy. Meaning, we will either expect our spouse to be perfect, or we will view them as a sinner who has been saved by grace. We are all fallen, yet we have an idea of how things should be. We can conceive of, or picture, what the ideal form of a situation should look like. We have an image of what the perfect husband/wife looks like in our minds. So, we can either view our spouse from the seat of judgment, looking down on them, or from the seat of mercy, looking up to Jesus. No one is perfect but Jesus.

To view your spouse from the judgment seat is to hold them accountable to that picture of perfection in your mind. If you are constantly criticizing and pointing out their flaws, you are sitting in the judgment seat. This is hypocritical because you are holding your spouse to a standard of perfection that you can't live up to yourself. Thus, you are living beneath your own criticisms. Choosing the seat of judgment will cause you to resent your spouse because they will constantly be falling short of perfection. On the other hand, you can choose to view your spouse from the seat of mercy; meaning you will choose to view them from a position of humility. To sit in the seat of mercy means you are quick to forgive. It is to exhibit unconditional love. It means you choose to build up your spouse and encourage them, when you could have torn them down. Viewing your spouse from a position of mercy will breed intimacy and foster a deeper connection. To sit in the seat of mercy means that you are aware of your own imperfections and you recognize that Jesus has forgiven you of many things. In turn, you extend that same grace and mercy to your spouse. This will allow you to celebrate their growth in the Lord as they become the man or woman that God created them to be.

MAKING YOUR PREFERENCE SPIRITUAL

For ye are yet carnal: for whereas there is among you envying, and strife, and divisions, are ye not carnal, and walk as men?
(1 Corinthians 3:3)

Another way preference can lead us into the seat of criticism is by allowing our personal preference to become a spiritual mandate. For the sake of argument, let us say that I prefer traditional hymns in a church worship setting. You may prefer contemporary worship music. Just because you do not agree with my preference does not make you more or less spiritual.

Often times Christian's try to give their own preferences more weight by adding, "God told me..." to a sentence. I honestly cannot remember how many times I have been told, "God told me..." In most cases, this was the result of a person trying to add weight to their personal preference. From members showing up at the office with some CD's with songs that they wanted sung, to those who have given me written sermons to preach—I've seen it all! I once was told that God did not honor a dedication service because I was not wearing white gloves. One man told me he would not attend our church because the church covenant was not framed on the wall on the right side of the pulpit. When I asked him what the "church covenant" stated, he could not tell me. This was something he had grown up seeing; and seeking to find fault, he pointed to that. I made my mind up years ago that I would not give my mind or energy to criticism that was not Biblical and Spirit-led. I am not saying that I am above criticism—I certainly am not. I am who I am by God's grace; but I will not allow anyone's criticism influence my life in a negative way.

Through the years, I have had members try to leverage my position of leadership. In an assembly of many people, it is impossible to please all. Some have come to me with their personal preferences. There are some that prefer a certain singer, song, leader, message, small group, etc. The sad thing is when those whose preferences are not catered to, they threaten to leave. Just because you prefer something to be a certain way does not make it righteous. We all have the potential of allowing our own selfish ambitions or feelings interrupt and cloud the right mindset. I have witnessed people overlook the result while they criticized the method. Jesus met this type of scrutiny throughout His ministry. We will look at examples later.

We would all do well to take a spiritual inventory of our beliefs and convictions and then be willing to weigh them against the Bible. If we were honest with ourselves, would we find any of our convictions to be more traditional rather than God-given or Bible-based? Only a person with a pure heart and a desire for the truth would be willing to do this. Sadly, many would rather hold on to what they have always known. They are unwilling to honestly search out what the Bible says because it may mean denying what they have long held as truth. I am convinced that if we would spend more time searching what God [His Word] says about a certain topic as we do what man has said, we would come to a different conclusion. Jesus said that we make the word of God of none effect through our tradition (Mark 7:13).

When I was saved in my teen years, I was attending a church that was very traditional. We sang hymns, and I had never witnessed a hand raised in worship or anything other than a hearty "amen" during a sermon. I remember an occasion where I visited an inter-denominational youth fellowship. I was standing next to a young woman who began to raise her hands during the worship service in addition to others who began to clap during certain songs of praise. My thought was, "This girl is only trying to draw attention to herself. She should put her hands down." Later in my walk of faith, I began to see that God's Word endorsed such acts in worship (Psalm 134:2). There was nothing wrong with the young woman raising her hands in worship—I was the one with the issue. My preference led me to falsely judge and accuse a fellow sister in Christ. I had never met her, nor did I know her heart; yet I cast judgment solely based on my personal preference (that would eventually be changed by the Word of God). This is a perfect example of where I had allowed my tradition to trump the Word of God.

As the pastor of an integrated church, I see this exemplified on a regular basis in the form of racism. In the South, many are accustomed to attending a church with an all-black or all-white congregation. You would not believe the criticism that comes against integrated churches. These critics are influenced by a racist mindset that the Bible does not support. The Word of God says that there is only one race—the human race. Acts 17:26 declares that God has "made of one blood all nations of men for to dwell on the face of the earth." We are all created equally and in the image of God (Genesis 1:26-27). Jesus died for all mankind.

> *For this is good and acceptable in the sight of God our Saviour; **Who will have all men to be saved**, and to come unto the knowledge of the truth. For there is one God, and one mediator between God and men, the man Christ Jesus;*

*Who gave himself a ransom for **all**, to be testified in due time* (1 Timothy 2:3-6, emphasis added).

This is only one of many Scriptures in the Bible that speak to this issue of racism. If you cannot handle an integrated congregation, you are going to have a hard time in an integrated Heaven. The truth is Heaven will have people of all backgrounds, from every nation, tongue, and ethnic group. Revelation 5:9 records the integrated scene of heaven as we sing the song of the redeemed, *"for thou wast slain, and hast redeemed us to God by thy blood out of every kindred, and tongue, and people, and nation."* The church should reflect Heaven. You would be hard pressed to find anything in the Bible that supports a racist mentality. If you cannot move beyond that critical and judgmental mindset, that is on you; but do not impose that on others.

I have had those with a prejudice mindset approach me for years. They have a list of things that they do not like about our assembly. I can always tell when their criticism is truly linked to racism. I had a minister (who is now a member) approach me about why he attended our church. He told me that he literally visited to find fault so that he could preach against our church from his pulpit. He told me that he was so overwhelmed by the love of the people and the Word of God that he decided to join. Thankfully his critical spirit was broken and his heart became receptive to truth. I am not saying that every critic should join our church. I only site this instance to convey the depth of criticism. There will be those whose personal preference will lead them to seek to find fault, criticize, and even destroy. Nevertheless, the Spirit of God is greater than the spirit of criticism.

Maybe you are on the receiving end of someone else's spiritual preference. Just because someone says, "God told me to tell you..." does not always mean God actually told him or her to tell you anything. I am not negating the fact that God speaks through others. He can certainly speak to us through others. However, the Bible gives parameters for this as a sort of filter, or safety net. You should always filter what is said through the Word of God. If God uses someone to speak to you, it will always be in line with His Word. If it contradicts the Bible, it is merely that person's preference, which they are trying to make sound spiritual in order to give it more weight. You are not obligated to cater to it. Godly counsel should always line up with God's Word. Some may even site Scripture, yet their heart, motives, and intentions are not pure. My point is that we should not spiritualize our preference and then become critical because our selfish desires were not duplicated or modeled in the other person's life.

It is impossible to cater to everyone's preference. We are called to please God and to stay in line with His word. Pleasing people is bondage. We cannot be caught up in it. We have an obligation to please God, our spouse, and family. Everyone has an opinion, and trying to please them all will only lead to bondage.

It is important to discern our personal preferences from what the Bible actually says on that subject. The Word of God is the only foundation by which we may rightly make judgments. When we start criticizing based on our own preference, we move out of the will of God.

I have been criticized for certain sermons that I have preached. Literally, in the same day, I heard testimony of lives that were blessed and others who were angered by the same message. I hear from those who are blessed by our worship services and others have said they would leave if I did not change the worship. I had one woman tell me that she would not attend our church because she heard we did not have a choir. I have had countless others commend the worship led by our worship pastor and praise team. At the end of the day, I have to recognize that everyone has a preference. My responsibility is to please God in my leadership. It is impossible to please everyone.

PREFERENCE THAT LEADS TO JEALOUSY

So then neither is he that planteth any thing, neither he that watereth; but God that giveth the increase (1 Corinthians 3:7).

You will recall from earlier that *preference* is partly defined as "an advantage that is given to some people but not others." Sometimes a critical spirit takes root in our lives through the avenue of fear. We become fearful that preference, or position, will be given to someone other than us. That fear manifests itself as jealousy.

For example. Say that you have a church with one piano but two piano players. Mrs. Jones feels she should be playing as lead pianist. Therefore, in her mind, Mrs. Smith is not cutting it. It is not that Mrs. Smith is not gifted. Mrs. Jones' criticism is based on jealousy—she wants that position. [These are names I am using for the sake of an illustration—not actual members.]

Don't let your life become infected by jealousy. There is no need for it. You have a heavenly Father who loves you and is mindful of you. There is no need you have that He cannot meet. He does not show preference. We all have equal access to His promises by faith. He has offered them and it is up to us to take hold of them.

Then Peter opened his mouth, and said, of a truth I perceive that God is no respecter of persons: But in every nation he that feareth him, and worketh righteousness, is accepted with him (Acts 10:34-35).

For there is no respect of persons with God (Romans 2:11).

On several occasions, the Bible makes the correlation between judgment and jealousy. The verse above says that God does not show favoritism. In the verses leading up to that one, the same connection is made:

> *Therefore thou art inexcusable, O man, whosoever thou art that judgest: for wherein thou judgest another, thou condemnest thyself; for thou that judgest doest the same things. But we are sure that the judgment of God is according to truth against them which commit such things. And thinkest thou this, O man, that judgest them which do such things, and doest the same, that thou shalt escape the judgment of God? Or despisest thou the riches of his goodness and forbearance and longsuffering; not knowing that the goodness of God leadeth thee to repentance? But after thy hardness and impenitent heart treasurest up unto thyself wrath against the day of wrath and revelation of the righteous judgment of God* (Romans 2:1-5).

To paraphrase, this is saying, who do you think you are to be jealous of someone else's good fortune? Do you not believe that God has a purpose in it? I love how the Amplified version explains it: "*Are you unmindful or actually ignorant of the fact that God's kindness is intended to lead you to repent? By your callous stubbornness [aka jealousy] you are storing up wrath and indignation for yourself...*" [emphasis added].

Jesus, in His infinite wisdom, knew that there was a connection between criticism, judgment, and jealousy. In the opening chapter of this book, we looked at the Sermon on the Mount, particularly Jesus' words on judgment. He goes on to address why there is no need for jealousy in the next five verses.

Ask, and it shall be given you; seek, and ye shall find; knock, and it shall be opened unto you: For every one that asketh receiveth; and he that seeketh findeth; and to him that knocketh it shall be opened. Or what man is there of you, whom if his son ask bread, will he give him a stone? Or if he ask a fish, will he give him a serpent? If ye then, being evil, know how to give good gifts unto your children, how much more shall your Father which is in heaven give good things to them that ask him? (Matthew 7:7-11).

He is saying is that there is no need for us to become jealous of each other. We would not give our children a rock if they asked us for bread. We love them and want to give them good things. In the same way, God love us and wants to give us good things. We need only to ask. It eliminates the need for jealousy. When you understand this, it makes you free to enjoy and celebrate the promotion of others. We have to rest in the sovereign power of an Almighty God. He has a plan for our lives. His will for us is peace and not evil and to give us an expected end (See Jeremiah 29:11).

CHOOSE LIFE

Nothing good comes from a jealous heart. A classic example of this is found in the story of Cain and Abel.

And Abel was a keeper of sheep, but Cain was a tiller of the ground. And in process of time it came to pass, that Cain brought of the fruit of the ground an offering unto the Lord. And Abel, he also brought of the firstlings of his flock and of the fat thereof. And the Lord had respect unto Abel and to his offering: But unto Cain and to his offering he had not respect. And Cain was very wroth, and his countenance fell. And the Lord said unto Cain, Why art thou wroth? and why is thy countenance fallen? If thou doest well, shalt thou not be accepted? and if thou doest not well, sin lieth at the door. And unto thee shall be his desire, and thou shalt rule over him. And Cain talked with Abel his brother: and it came to pass, when they were in the field, that Cain rose up against Abel his brother, and slew him. And the Lord said unto Cain, Where is Abel thy brother? And he said, I know not: Am I my brother's keeper? And he said, What hast thou done? the voice of thy brother's blood crieth unto me from the ground. And now art thou cursed from the earth, which hath opened her mouth to receive thy brother's blood from thy hand (Genesis 4:2-11).

God did show preference to Abel's offering, but it was not arbitrary. Reading in context shows us how their offerings contrasted. Cain gave "in the process of time," whereas Able gave the "firstlings." More importantly, Cain brought the Lord the product of his own work, whereas Abel brought God an offering of faith (a blood sacrifice). That is why God respected Abel's offering. You have to think, Cain and Abel were the sons of Adam and Eve who had walked with God and heard His Word. They would have known that He is a God of faith, and would have passed that knowledge along to their children. We can see that this is the case because it is implied in what God told Cain. Surely, they had heard the story of how God sacrificed an animal (I believe a lamb) as a covering for Adam and Eve's sin. Cain would have had to know the power of a blood sacrifice, just as his younger brother Abel did.

Cain was upset and God basically told him, *"Why are you upset? You know if you do well* [or if you amend your offering to what you know it should be] *you will also be accepted."* Could it be that Cain's pride got in the way of his submission to God? It seems that is exactly what happened. Instead of doing the right thing, he persisted in going the wrong direction. Instead of taking God's advice, he got angrier and killed his brother. That is the apex of jealousy—envy. (I will deal with envy more directly later in this book.) Jealousy begins with a fear of a loss of attention, affection or preference. Envy is when you seek to destroy the one of whom you are jealous. Because of jealousy and envy, Cain got a curse that was more than he could bear. Because of his stubbornness, he brought down judgment on himself. I often wonder if Cain's bitter heart had more to do with not wanting his brother to feel he was right than having his own heart being right toward God. This is pride showing up in the form of preference. It is a heart that refuses to be wrong; or more so, accept that another is right.

Next time you feel jealousy rear its ugly head, remember that you have the same choice as Cain did. You can 'do well' by keeping God's commandments and take hold of His promises by faith, or you can allow jealousy to persist. You are free to choose; but you are not free from the consequences of your choice. We choose the seed we sow and the seed we sow determines the harvest. If you so choose to constantly bombard your spouse with criticisms, don't be alarmed by the harvest that will yield in your marriage. Our words and actions should be treated like seed. Sow what you want to reap!

I call heaven and earth to record this day against you, that I have set before you life and death, blessing and cursing: therefore choose life, that both thou and thy seed may live: That thou mayest love the Lord thy God, and that thou mayest obey his voice, and that thou mayest cleave unto him: for he is thy life, and the length of thy days (Deuteronomy 30:19-20).

Before we move forward to the next point, let us solidify this one. Preference is a source of criticism. Are you becoming critical of something or others based on personal preference? If so, make a decision to denounce it. Do not try to spiritualize the thing you simply prefer.

I recently met a sweet elderly woman in the foyer of our church. She informed me that when she first visited she was taken by our worship services. She told me she had never experienced such an atmosphere and was initially critical. She went on to say that, once she entered the sanctuary, she could not hold back the tears from the overwhelming presence of the Spirit of God! Here was an older woman who was about to miss out on something God had for her all because of preference. However, she broke through and had a break-through! Do not spiritualize your preferences and allow it to turn you into a prideful critic. Just because you don't prefer something does not necessarily make it wrong. Preferences change in time—let us not spiritualize them to criticize others.

Chapter 4

RESENTMENT

The word resentment is defined as a feeling of anger or displeasure about someone or something unfair (Merriam-Webster.com). Resentment can also mean to take ill, to consider as an injury or affront, or to be in some degree angry or provoked (1828 Webster's Dictionary).

There are two main reasons we begin to resent someone: misunderstanding and unforgiveness. You will be critical of those you resent. Resentment, if left unchecked, can spiritually cripple a person.

Just as calloused hands are less sensitive to the use of a tool, resentment causes our hearts to become less sensitive to the convicting voice of God's Spirit. God wants us to have a soft heart that is sensitive to His voice. Resentment is like a callous that grows and grows in the heart until eventually it can feel nothing. The heart of a calloused person will not be receptive to God's voice.

Sadly, the person holding the resentment is the one that suffers most. In their eyes, the one they resent can do no right. This critical spirit will lead you down a slippery slope of misery. I have witnessed individuals become literally obsessed with those they resent. They will examine their every move only hoping to find something to criticize. I have seen resentment lead people to begin to criticize everything associated with the one they resent. Imagine the example I gave earlier of the two piano players in the same church. If Mrs. Jones is allowed to play during a special program, Mrs. Smith may not only become critical of Mrs. Jones' piano playing, but also become critical of the entire program. She might even refuse to attend. If it cannot be her, then she refuses to participate. Though this is only an example, I have seen this literally in other areas of ministry.

A much weightier example of resentment can be found in marriage. If you hold unforgiveness in your heart toward your spouse it will lead to resentment. Your resentment will cause you to become critical of their every move. If left unchecked, one can literally devastate the marriage and strip it of life and joy. Nothing good can come from a relationship where there is resentment. The answer is the freedom that comes through true forgiveness.

Make a decision today to walk free from resentment. Do not let the injuries of your past torment your present and sabotage your future. Release your resentment through forgiveness and be free in Jesus name!

RESENTMENT TOWARDS GOD

Because the present state of the world is fallen, we will all encounter some type of pain in life. It is unavoidable. The key is not to let your anger drive you to bitter resentment. Ruth and Naomi are great examples of resentment over-comers! In the book of Ruth, we read that Naomi had lost her husband and two sons. Understandably, she had taken on a depressed demeanor. This is especially obvious when she asked her daughters-in-law to stop calling her "Naomi" (meaning "pleasant") and start calling her "Mara" (meaning "bitter"). She goes on to say:

For the Almighty hath dealt very bitterly with me. I went out full and the Lord hath brought me home again empty: why then call ye me Naomi, seeing the Lord hath testified against me, and the Almighty hath afflicted me? (Ruth 1:20-21).

Naomi was faced with a choice. She could stay bitter or turn to God in faith. I love this story because it is a great example of how God can turn any situation around and work it out for our good and His glory. We go on to find that because of Ruth's devotion, Naomi decides to take the repentance route. She ends up becoming the nurse to Ruth's son, who was the grandfather of King David—in the lineage of Jesus!

Resentment is a trap that tempts us to believe God does not have our best interest at heart. When we are faced with feelings of resentment, we need to press into God and build up our faith. I have known individuals who began to resent God for (perceived) unanswered prayer, the death of a loved one or the feeling of abandonment. The resentful soul becomes critical of God, the Bible, church, and preachers. A resentful person's heart becomes hardened to the message of faith and trust. The enemy would love for us to become critical of God through resentment.

I remember when my mom was in I.C.U. shortly before her passing. I was standing in faith for her healing. I would visit her bed at every opportunity and pray over her. My family witnessed my steadfast faith. I refused to speak anything but life, nor would I accept any report but healing. On April 8, 2008, my mom went to be with the Lord. I later heard that there were some that were literally concerned about me the moment my mom passed. Their thought was that I would turn bitter at God. When a loved one asked me how I had accepted my mom's death so well, I informed her that my mom was in a win-win position. If the Lord healed her, we would have more time. If not, she was going to be with Jesus and would never suffer again! The thing is, I may have prayed in faith—but how do I know my mom wasn't asking the Lord to take her home?

On the morning she passed God worked a miracle. Momma and I had a supernatural visit. She had not been conscious for days; but on the morning that she passed, I was able to visit with her alert and awake. I remember telling her that the Lord was with her and she need not fear. She shook her head in agreement. I then said, "But you're more concerned about me aren't you?" She nodded. I told her that the Lord would take care of me. That was the last conversation I had with my mom. Do you think the enemy would want me to resent God for not giving mother more time? Absolutely! But, as I told my loved ones, there comes a time when we shift our faith into trust. We must trust God. We will never understand it all. Presently we see through a glass darkly. However, one day we will see face to face!

Another great Biblical example of trust trumping resentment is found in the story of Daniel. Calamity had come over the land. Because of Israel's rebellion, things were not looking good. Daniel prays on behalf of Jerusalem a prayer of repentance to God, asking Him to turn away His wrath and to have mercy. He has a somewhat terrifying vision. Things appeared to be getting worse. For three weeks, Daniel chose to hold fast to his faith rather than give up hope. His prayers are answered.

Therefore I was left alone, and saw this great vision, and there remained no strength in me: for my comeliness was turned in me into corruption, and I retained no strength. Yet heard I the voice of his words: and when I heard the voice of his words, then was I in a deep sleep on my face, and my face toward the ground. And, behold, an hand touched me, which set me upon my knees and upon the palms of my hands. And he said unto me, O Daniel, a man greatly beloved, understand the words that I speak unto thee, and stand upright: for unto thee am I now sent. And when he had spoken this word unto me, I stood trembling. Then said he unto me, Fear not, Daniel: for from the first day that thou didst set thine heart to understand, and to chasten thyself before thy God, thy words were heard, and I am come for thy words. But the prince of the kingdom of Persia withstood me one and twenty days: but, lo, Michael, one of the chief princes, came to help me; and I remained there with the kings of Persia. Now I am come to make thee understand what shall befall thy people in the latter days: for yet the vision is for many days (Daniel 10:8-14).

Though Daniel's understanding of his predicament was delayed, it was on the way from the moment he asked for it. God also made sure that Daniel's strength was restored.

Then there came again and touched me one like the appearance of a man, and he strengthened me, And said, O man greatly beloved, fear not: peace be unto thee, be strong, yea, be strong. And when he had spoken unto me, I was strengthened, and said, Let my lord speak; for thou hast strengthened me (Daniel 10:18-19).

Things looked bad. Daniel could have given into resentment. Instead, he chose to hold on to his faith. He added trust to his faith. It paid off!

Often resentment is born out of offense. There are two types of offended people: those who have been wronged and those who think that they have been wronged. Offense is rooted in unfulfilled expectations. When we allow offense to set in, it can lead to resentment. This resentment might be towards God (for not answering your prayer the way you expected) or others. In either case, we must choose to forgive, forget and walk in love. After all, love is the greatest enemy to offense.

RESENTMENT TOWARDS OTHERS

So likewise shall my heavenly Father do also unto you, if ye from your hearts forgive not every one his brother their trespasses (Matthew 18:35).

Harboring resentment towards other people will affect us the same way as harboring resentment towards God. Resentment itself is a bad seed. Holding onto resentment is like allowing poison to remain in your body— it is the gall of bitterness (See Acts 8:23).

Many times children are caught in a conflict of resentment between parents who have divorced and remarried. A child will go to spend the weekend with his father and stepmother. When he returns home his mother asks, "How was your weekend? Did you eat well?" The child tells his mother that his stepmother made spaghetti. The mother replies, "I bet her spaghetti isn't as good as mine. Of course she made spaghetti. She can't cook anything better." It was not the food that the mother is criticizing. The real issue is the resentment the mother has for the father and stepmother. What this mother may not realize is that child is learning to act how she acts. If she does not train him to be better, he will grow up crippled by the same resentful mindset she allowed to stay in her heart.

Resentment often latches on to petty things and magnifies them. Do not allow yourself to be a tool of the enemy. Do not be the perpetuation of a generational curse. Not only are you hurting yourself, you are negatively affecting others who are involved. Resentment is not good for you. It will affect your life and health. Through my years of pastoring, I have witnessed individuals carry resentments from the past into their present relationships. Here are a few examples: The man who carries the resentment of a previous relationship into a new one; The wife who carries the resentment towards her father into a marriage with her husband; The believer who carries a resentment towards a minister into a new church assembly. (And the list could on and on.)

Once we have resentment towards someone, he or she can do no right in our eyes. Everything about that person is filtered through our resentment towards them. While at the same time, it is causing our heart to grow more calloused. It is not of God. However, it is never too late to repent and forgive. Restoration is waiting for any who ask for it!

If my people, which are called by my name, shall humble themselves, and pray, and seek my face, and turn from their wicked ways; then will I hear from heaven, and will forgive their sin, and will heal their land. Now mine eyes shall be open, and mine ears attent unto the prayer that is made in this place. For now have I chosen and sanctified this house, that my name may be there for ever: and mine eyes and mine heart shall be there perpetually (2 Chronicles 7:14-16).

Repent ye therefore, and be converted, that your sins may be blotted out, when the times of refreshing shall come from the presence of the Lord (Acts 3:19).

If we confess our sins, he is faithful and just to forgive us our sins, and to cleanse us from all unrighteousness (1 John 1:9).

Bring forth therefore fruits meet for repentance (Matthew 3:8).

For thus saith the Lord God, the Holy One of Israel; In returning and rest shall ye be saved; in quietness and in confidence shall be your strength... (Isaiah 30:15).

From that time Jesus began to preach, and to say, Repent: for the kingdom of heaven is at hand (Matthew 4:17).

Chapter 5

INFERIORITY

◆

Inferiority is a belief that you are less worthy or less important than other people are. Though it may sound contradictory, feelings of inferiority can actually stem from a prideful mindset. In this chapter, we will take a deeper look at the relationship of pride, inferiority, and criticism.

King Saul, whose name means *desired*, portrays one of the Bible's greatest examples of inferior pride. Saul's story also shows how feelings of inferiority can lead to a critical spirit. His name gives us somewhat of an idea about the kind of person he was and the things that were important to him. The Bible calls him *"a choice young man, and goodly [handsome]: and there was not among the children of Israel a goodlier person than he: from his shoulders and upward he was higher than any of the people"* (1 Samuel 9:2, emphasis added). Here we have a handsome young man from a wealthy family who is described as taller and better looking than all the people in Israel. Is it possible that Saul saw himself in the same manner, with a hint of vanity?

God sent His prophet Samuel to anoint Saul and give him the title of king. In the beginning of his journey, Saul showed reverence and obedience to God. However, as he got used to being king and the glory that came with it, his obedience started to wane. Saul's reputation had grown favorably because God gave him victory as he battled all the other nations who had troubled Israel in the past. Saul became a type of war-hero among his soldiers, a good feeling no doubt. True to his prideful nature, he began to forget that it was God who handed him all of those victories.

Evidence of this is clearly seen when he blatantly disobeyed God's commandments concerning the Amalekites—the people who had fought against Moses and the Israelites as they came out of Egypt. Because of this evil, God told Saul to destroy them. He was told specifically not to let any live, not even the animals.

> *Thus saith the Lord of hosts, I remember that which Amalek did to Israel, how he laid wait for him in the way, when he came up from Egypt. Now go and smite Amalek, and utterly destroy all that they have, and spare them not; but slay both man and woman, infant and suckling, ox and sheep, camel and ass* (1 Samuel 15:2-3).

Partial obedience is not obedience. Saul did not listen to this commandment. He destroyed all of the people but he saved the king and the best of the spoils. Why would Saul spare Agag, the king of the Amalekites? It is likely that he viewed Agag as a sort of war trophy that he could show off as testament to his power. This disobedience cost him.

> *And he took Agag the king of the Amalekites alive, and utterly destroyed all the people with the edge of the sword. But Saul and the people spared Agag, and the best of the sheep, and of the oxen, and of the fatlings, and the lambs, and all that was good, and would not utterly destroy them: but every thing that was vile and refuse, that they destroyed utterly.*

Then came the word of the Lord unto Samuel, saying, It repenteth me that I have set up Saul to be king: for he is turned back from following me, and hath not performed my commandments. And it grieved Samuel; and he cried unto the Lord all night.

And when Samuel rose early to meet Saul in the morning, it was told Samuel, saying, Saul came to Carmel, and, behold, he set him up a place, and is gone about, and passed on, and gone down to Gilgal.

And Samuel came to Saul: and Saul said unto him, Blessed be thou of the Lord: I have performed the commandment of the Lord. And Samuel said, What meaneth then this bleating of the sheep in mine ears, and the lowing of the oxen which I hear? (1 Samuel 15:8-14).

Pride is a deceiver that keeps us from seeing things as they really are. It makes us start to believe that our way is better than God's way. Saul allowed pride to take root in his heart and influence his actions. When confronted with his wrongs, he tried to blame his soldiers and his people. It ultimately costs him God's anointing.

What does this have to do with feelings of inferiority and criticism? Saul's story does not end there. Pride is a stepping-stone to inferiority, which in turn, leads to criticism.

The next man God chose to become king was David. Right away, it is clear that David was different from Saul. He was the youngest and weakest looking of the eight sons of Jesse. God instructed His prophet Samuel to go to the house of Jesse where he would find the next chosen king.

Samuel must have been thinking that God would do as He did with Saul and choose a sturdy looking man. When he surveys the house of Jesse, he goes to the tallest son and thinks, "This has to be the one God chosen." The Lord told Samuel, "*Look not on his countenance, or on the height of his stature: because I have refused him: for the Lord seeth not as man seeth: for man looketh on the outward appearance, but the Lord looketh on the heart*" (1 Samuel 16:7).

As it turns out, none of the sons in the line-up was the chosen one. No one would have thought David would be a candidate for king. His own father did not even think to bring him in before Samuel for consideration. After God refused all seven of the older brothers, Samuel was left scratching his head. He asks Jesse, "*Is this all of your sons?*" Jesse was probably thinking, "Well there is David, but surely God didn't choose him!" The Bible describes David as *ruddy* or reddish looking. His job was to keep the family's sheep. Leave it to God to take the foolish things of the world to confound the wise. It was David who God had chosen; and on that day, he was anointed with God's Spirit and appointed the next to become king.

Pride is a blinder. It makes a person unable to understand the things of the Spirit. A proud person would not understand why God would choose someone who appears less adequate. They will never understand why the meek are blessed. The boaster in spirit cannot see why the poor in spirit inherit the Kingdom (See Matthew 5:3). Saul may not have seen God's wisdom in choosing David as his next anointed king, but he did feel the loss of God's anointing on his life. Though he was still king, he no longer had God's anointing. God's Spirit departed from Saul and was replaced by a tormenting spirit, one that tormented Saul frequently.

Though David had not yet taken his position as king, he did have God's powerful anointing. It was evident to all as he began doing mighty things. David became armor-bearer in Saul's army. He also had the ability to play the lyre in a way that would drive the tormenting spirits away from Saul. Because of this, Saul came to love him. However, that love quickly turned into something else.

This is where *inferiority* and *criticism* enter the picture.

One day Saul and his armies were camped across from the Philistines who had been threatening them. For forty days Goliath, a particularly scary looking Philistine, had been challenging someone from Saul's army to fight him. All of Saul's men were too afraid to make a move. Meanwhile, David was sent by his father to the campground to bring provisions to his brothers. While he is there, he sees what is going on and asks, *"What shall be done to the man that killeth this Philistine, and taketh away the reproach from Israel? for who is this uncircumcised Philistine, that he should defy the armies of the living God?"* (1 Samuel 17:26).

Apparently, no one had much faith in David. His own brother accused him of being mischievous and only coming out to see the fight. David offered to go and fight Goliath himself. Saul tried to stop him, listing all the reasons why David would lose. David would not be deterred. He never faltered from his cause. Naturally, the fight looked completely in Goliath's favor. He was a skilled man of war while David had no war experience. When David stepped up to fight, Goliath literally balked and felt insulted. As he laid eyes on David, he said, *"Am I a dog, that thou comest to me with staves?"* (1 Samuel 17:43).

Despite all the opposition and lack of support, David knew the Lord was on his side. He spoke his victory before it happened.

Thou comest to me with a sword, and with a spear, and with a shield: but I come to thee in the name of the Lord of hosts, the God of the armies of Israel, whom thou hast defied. This day will the Lord deliver thee into mine hand; and I will

smite thee, and take thine head from thee; and I will give the
carcases of the host of the Philistines this day unto the fowls
of the air, and to the wild beasts of the earth; that all the
earth may know that there is a God in Israel. And all this
assembly shall know that the Lord saveth not with sword
and spear: for the battle is the Lord's, and he will give you
into our hands (1 Samuel 17:45-47).

Not only did David kill the giant Goliath with a sling and a stone, but also he sent the entire Philistine army running in fear! Because of this, Saul's pride was wounded. Before this incident, he had been fond of David. Now he was becoming wary of him. He had even offered David his armor. Sometimes those who feel inferior offer their support only so they can boast in their contributions to our victories. At this point, the relationship between David and King Saul began to shift.

David and Saul's son, Jonathan, became friends. They won numerous battles together and became famous among the people. It was quickly becoming obvious that David was surpassing Saul's earlier battle victories. Again, Saul's pride caused him to become more and more enraged. The fame of battle from his earlier days was pretty much all Saul had left. It was the only thing giving some credence to his kingship. Now David was outperforming him and he did not like it.

And Saul was very wroth, and the saying displeased him;
and he said, They have ascribed unto David ten thousands,
and to me they have ascribed but thousands: and what can
he have more but the kingdom? And Saul eyed David from
that day and forward (1 Samuel 18:8-9).

Take note of the change in Saul's attitude after his pride is wounded. He has gone from loving David to being judgmental and critical of him. All because people were saying that David had killed more enemies than Saul.

Saul becomes plagued with *inferiority*. That made him become *critical*.

Saul began a subtle campaign against David. Knowing that David was not rich, and had no dowry money, Saul offered his daughter to David in marriage. It was a trap.

> *And Saul's servants spoke those words in the ears of David. And David said, "Does it seem to you a little thing to become the king's son-in-law, since I am a poor man and have no reputation?" And the servants of Saul told him, "Thus and so did David speak." Then Saul said, "Thus shall you say to David, 'The king desires no bride-price except a hundred foreskins of the Philistines, that he may be avenged of the king's enemies.'" Now Saul thought to make David fall by the hand of the Philistines. And when his servants told David these words, it pleased David well to be the king's son-in-law. Before the time had expired, David arose and went, along with his men, and killed two hundred of the Philistines. And David brought their foreskins, which were given in full number to the king, that he might become the king's son-in-law* (1 Samuel 18:23-27).

Saul gave David a seemingly impossible task. Hoping to get David killed, Saul told him that he would not have to pay a dowry in order to marry his daughter. He would only be required to kill and dismember 200 Philistines. When David surprised him and succeeded, Saul became even more enraged. Not only was David not dead, but the Bible says that his name became highly esteemed. Saul's plan turned against him.

Eventually Saul's criticism drove him to attempt to murder David. It is sad really. Saul was a man who started out as king, anointed by God, and with God's favor. Because of his pride and inferiority, he was reduced to a washed up king obsessed with killing David. Like Satan, Saul's pride caused him to fall a long way. He failed in his attempts on David's life and eventually dishonorably lost his own life.

The story of Saul shows what a slippery slope pride can be if we allow it to remain in us. Inferiority is a type of injured pride that leads to criticism. Do not let inferiority take root in your life and do not be surprised that your worst critics are moved by inferiority to you.

The injured pride of inferiority seeks to diminish others. This diminishing through criticism is not genuine. The inferior person will tear others down for the sake of making themselves look better. The constant demeaning of another is rooted in low self-esteem and inferiority. You are uniquely and wonderfully made. There is never a reason to tear another down for the motive of self-promotion.

COUNTERFEIT TO EXCELLENCE

It pleased Darius to set over the kingdom an hundred and twenty princes, which should be over the whole kingdom; And over these three presidents; of whom Daniel was first: that the princes might give accounts unto them, and the king should have no damage. Then this Daniel was preferred above the presidents and princes, because an excellent spirit was in him; and the king thought to set him over the whole realm. Then the presidents and princes sought to find occasion against Daniel concerning the kingdom; but they could find none occasion nor fault; forasmuch as he was faithful, neither was there any error or fault found in him (Daniel 6:1-4).

In the story quoted above, we see that Daniel operated by the spirit of excellence. This excellent spirit caused him to be "preferred" (Daniel 6:3). Notice that because he was preferred, his peers attempted to find fault with him (v. 4). Operating in excellence, which leads to preference, will cause others to become critical of you. We looked at preference being the first root of criticism. We can see in this story how inferiority played a role as well. Daniel's excellence made certain people around him feel inferior. This led them to attempt to bring him down in order to make themselves look better. You might be surprised to learn that your worst critic actually feels inferior to you. Some will simply try to hide their own lack of excellence with criticism.

Criticism is the counterfeit to excellence.

I have a strong conviction about excellence. I like my yard to be excellent. I like my house to be excellent. As a ministry, church and school, I want everything we do to be excellent. It is not always excellent, but it is my desire. When people come to Word of God Ministries, I want everything to be excellent. Just the other day I was driving by one of our campuses and noticed a light bulb on the building that was out. If I had had a ladder and bulb in my vehicle, I would have pulled over right then and changed it. I cannot take it with things are not excellent and in order.

Years ago, the Lord dealt with me about this. I was in prayer one night and the Lord laid this on my heart, *"Be careful that you don't let the spirit of excellence lead you into the spirit of criticism, because criticism is a counterfeit excellence."* It works like this: if I have not reached my potential or if I have not yet arrived at excellence, I may start to feel that I can appear to be excellent by being critical of others.

To illustrate, let's say you wanted to be starting quarterback in high school, but you never got past back-up quarterback. Because of this, your reaction to others as they play in the position is always critical. No one can play the position right in your eyes. Even years later, you refer to the time when you played ball (not mentioning that you were not personally successful). Could your reaction be counterfeit excellence? Is it possible that your criticism of everyone else in the game is a counterfeit type of excellence meant to make you look better than what you actually are? Are you in some way compensating for your lack of success? In other words, are you willing to highlight the faults of others to make yourself look good?

Maybe in your heart you always wanted to enter a certain occupation, profession, or ministry. Yet somehow, it never came to fruition. Now, feeling like you lost your dream opportunity, you begin to tear down those who are living the life you wanted. Since you never 'excelled' in a certain field, you find yourself overly critical of those who hold the position you always wanted. I have found that my worst critics are either ministers or those who desired to be in some form of ministry. When we do not feel like we have fulfilled or dreams or destiny, it can lead to inferiority. Inferiority can lead to criticism—especially towards those who are living the life we wanted for ourselves. Be on guard! Don't allow yourself to become critical of someone else simply because it appears they are living out your dream or desire. To everything there is a season (Ecclesiastes 3:1). Don't hinder your season because of your criticism of another's. Romans 12:15 declares, *"Rejoice with them that do rejoice, and weep with them that weep."* If another appears to be living out your dream, rejoice with them! In so doing, you plant seeds for your season!

As was evident with Saul, inferiority is an issue of self-esteem. It says, *"I'm not who I thought I would be and I haven't accomplished all that I thought I would have... so to cover all that up, I am critical of others who have."*

We find another example of this in Luke 13 when Jesus heals a woman as He is teaching in a synagogue on the Sabbath. Consider these verses,

> *And, behold, there was a woman which had a spirit of infirmity eighteen years, and was bowed together, and could in no wise lift up herself. And when Jesus saw her, he called her to him, and said unto her, Woman, thou art loosed from thine infirmity. And he laid his hands on her: and immediately she was made straight, and glorified God. And the ruler of the synagogue answered with indignation, because that Jesus had healed on the sabbath day, and said unto the people, There are six days in which men ought to work: in them therefore come and be healed, and not on the sabbath day* (Luke 13:10-14).

Jesus healed the woman and she glorified God. Because of this, the Pharisees were driven to indignation. They complained that He should not heal on the Sabbath day. They had to find something wrong with what Jesus had done. I believe they were driven by feelings of inferiority and resentment. They were operating in a counterfeit excellence. Jesus had to come back and set them straight, saying,

> *"Ought not this woman, being a daughter of Abraham, whom Satan hath bound, lo, these eighteen years, be loosed from this bond on the sabbath day?"* (Luke 13:16).

Surely, the Pharisees felt embarrassed, inferior and resentful of Jesus. This woman had been up under their leadership and teaching for eighteen years and had not been healed or made free. Basically, they could not do what Jesus did. Their only response was that 'they didn't work on the Sabbath day.' The power that Jesus portrayed brought to light the evident lack of power in the lives of the Pharisees, causing them to feel angry. To cover their inadequacies, they became critical. Likewise, there are many people today who have not accomplished anything, so they attack those who have. The Bible warns us against this.

> *But the tongue can no man tame; it is an unruly evil, full of deadly poison. Therewith bless we God, even the Father; and therewith curse we men, which are made after the similitude of God. Out of the same mouth proceedeth blessing and cursing. My brethren, these things ought not so to be* (James 3:8-10).

THE INFERIORITY COMPLEX

Personal strongholds and a negative spirit come from the feeling of inferiority. When inferiority is allowed to take root in our hearts, it leads to an inferiority complex. This is poisonous. It will negatively affect every area of your life and all of your relationships. It will cause you to be deceived and see things from the wrong mindset. Inferiority causes a negative attitude in us that can make us become critical of others.

Imagine that your neighbor buys a new vehicle, and in your heart, you are a little jealous. One day you see him outside and say, "Hey, that's a nice car. Did you get the six or eight cylinder?" When he replies, "The six," you respond, "You should have gotten the eight. It has more power."

Ask yourself, do you really care about what size engine is in the car? No. Inferiority leads us to tear down other's good in order to feel better about our own. Maybe your response was something like, "Yea, my cousin bought one exactly like that. But he got the bigger wheels." Why do we feel the need to 'one-up' people? Could it be that we are dealing with feelings of inferiority? The inferiority complex seeks to injure other's pride.

As Christians, it is so important that that we understand our value and identity in Christ. The Bible tells us that we are complete in Him (Colossians 2:10). It is always God's will that we be complete in Him. He does not want us to lack any good thing. (See James 1:3-4). Instead of allowing pride to take root, we should deal with it, knowing that God has good plans for us! Do not allow feelings of inferiority to cause you to become extra-critical of others. If you do not like where you are at, pray and seek God's help.

And we know that all things work together for good to them that love God, to them who are the called according to his purpose (Romans 8:28).

Fear God, and keep his commandments: for this is the whole duty of man. For God shall bring every work into judgment, with every secret thing, whether it be good, or whether it be evil (Ecclesiastes 12:13-14).

Whosoever believeth that Jesus is the Christ is born of God: and every one that loveth him that begat loveth him also that is begotten of him. By this we know that we love the children of God, when we love God, and keep his commandments. For this is the love of God, that we keep his commandments: and his commandments are not grievous. For whatsoever is born of God overcometh the world: and this is the victory that overcometh the world, even our faith (1 John 5:1-4).

Know therefore that the Lord thy God, he is God, the faithful God, which keepeth covenant and mercy with them that love him and keep his commandments to a thousand generations. Wherefore it shall come to pass, if ye hearken to these judgments, and keep, and do them, that the Lord thy God shall keep unto thee the covenant and the mercy which he sware unto thy fathers (Deuteronomy 7:9, 12).

Chapter 6

DEFENSIVENESS

A defense is meant to protect someone or something from attack, to help keep a person or thing safe. To act in a defensive way means to offer an explanation that frees one from fault or blame.

Defensiveness acts as a shield to our pride. Defensive people are always right in their own mind. A defensive person cannot take constructive criticism because he is never wrong. The fact is that God does corrects His children. The Bible says that whom the Lord loves, He corrects (Hebrews 12:6). To assume a defensive attitude means we are shielding our wrongdoings and ourselves. It is like trying to offer a justification or excuse to God. Making excuses to God is like telling Him that He does not know what is best for us and that He is not right in correcting us. If we choose to live this way, it will be hard to hear God and impossible to grow into spiritual maturity.

The Bible says that as Christians we are constantly growing. We should be in the process of becoming more like Jesus every day. This means we must change and conform to His image. It means that our lives should not look the same today as they did a week ago or a year ago. If we are growing in Christ-likeness then our lives will reflect greater fruit as our walk progresses. When we choose to become defensive, we are halting our growth. It is as if we are digging our heels in and refusing to walk any further with God.

None of us is beyond needing correction—we are all imperfect. God will correct us when we need it because He loves us. The Bible teaches this.

> *For whom the Lord loveth he chasteneth, and scourgeth every son whom he receiveth. If ye endure chastening, God dealeth with you as with sons; for what son is he whom the father chasteneth not? But if ye be without chastisement, whereof all are partakers, then are ye bastards, and not sons. Furthermore we have had fathers of our flesh which corrected us, and we gave them reverence: shall we not much rather be in subjection unto the Father of spirits, and live? For they verily for a few days chastened us after their own pleasure; but he for our profit, that we might be partakers of his holiness. Now no chastening for the present seemeth to be joyous, but grievous: nevertheless afterward it yieldeth the peaceable fruit of righteousness unto them which are exercised thereby* (Hebrews 12:6-11).

It does not feel good to be corrected. Just as Adam did when God confronted him, many of us want to defend ourselves. If we are willing to be honest with God and allow Him to correct us, it will help us in the end. The verse above says that though correction may be hard at the time, if we will allow it, it will end up producing Godly fruit in our lives. It says that God corrects us so that we can be more like Him, becoming partakers in His holiness. We have to trust that if we submit to God's correction, it will lead to a better life for us. Anything God wants to work out in us is always for our good!

Furthermore, this verse says that we would not be children of God if He did not chasten or correct us. Did your parents ever spank you? Many of you came from a different generation where children were taught to respect their parents. I knew better than to disrespect my daddy. Through his discipline, I learned to show him respect. Though I was disciplined as a child, I always felt that my dad loved me. One day I realized it was all for my good. There is a different perspective that comes with age and with having kids of your own. You realize how much discipline is motivated by love. You discipline your kids because you want them to learn how to succeed in life. You set boundaries to keep them safe and healthy. In the same way, God will correct us in order to make us more like Him so that we may succeed in our calling.

The Bible says that when we heed the Lords correction we are learning to walk in His ways. This will lead us to a life of health and abundance.

Trust in the Lord with all thine heart; and lean not unto thine own understanding. In all thy ways acknowledge him, and he shall direct thy paths. Be not wise in thine own eyes: fear the Lord, and depart from evil. It shall be health to thy navel, and marrow to thy bones. Honour the Lord with thy substance, and with the firstfruits of all thine increase: So shall thy barns be filled with plenty, and thy presses shall burst out with new wine. My son, despise not the chastening of the Lord; neither be weary of his correction: For whom the Lord loveth he correcteth; even as a father the son in whom he delighteth (Proverbs 3:5-12).

If we do not understand that God's correction is always motivated by love, we will not be open to it. It is vital to understand that God has a purpose in correcting us. Sometimes we are so quick to defend ourselves that we miss the reason for which the correction was needed. The Book of Proverbs calls this folly.

> *He that answereth a matter before he heareth it, it is folly*
> *and shame unto him* (Proverbs 18:13).

Trusting God is vital. Sometimes He will ask us to do difficult things. If we do not believe that they will be for our good, we will not obey Him. Sometimes He will ask us to do things we do not immediately understand. And, if we choose to defend ourselves, we will never see the bigger picture. God is all-knowing. He sees things we cannot yet see. If we lack faith and trust in Him, we will not obey Him. Obedience is essential if we want to walk in His perfect will for our lives. Do not let the temptation to be defensive keep you blind to the bigger picture. Do not let it keep you from progressing into the abundant life God wants to give you.

DEFENSIVENESS: HINDRANCE TO COMMUNICATION

I often tell the church that the quality of your life will never exceed the quality of your relationships. God made us to need Him and to need one another. Relationships require work. They are not perfect by default. We have to sow into them. This is especially true of marriage, where a defensive attitude can be a major issue and a hindrance to intimacy. A person who is defensive and easily offended will have a hard time in their relationship with God, and with their spouse, because sometimes intimacy means talking about difficult things. It is hard to talk to defensive people. If you take on a defensive attitude, you are essentially saying to your spouse, *"Don't bring your concerns to me. There isn't even a chance that I'm wrong, or that your concern with me has any merit."* It communicates the idea that, *"your feelings don't matter to me enough that I am willing to openly listen to what you have to say."*

If you are easily offended, you will alienate yourself and close the door to healthy communication with your spouse and with others. Do you really want to be the kind of person that people feel like they cannot talk to? Do you want people to feel like they have to walk on eggshells around you? This can be detrimental to any personal relationship and especially a marriage. For example, let's say something is bothering your spouse. You may sense something is wrong; you might even ask them about it. However, if you are a defensive and easily angered person, they will not open up to you about what is bothering them because they will not feel like they can talk to you. They will never bring any concerns to you for fear how you will respond. Without the ability to talk openly, problems would never get resolved. A defensive person will end up isolating himself or herself because their attitude puts off a vibe that says, *"You better not bring your concerns to me or I will lose my cool with you."*

A defensive attitude can easily lead to a critical spirit. Have you ever had an argument with your spouse that started with a small concern but ended up in a blame battle? A defensive person will meet *constructive* criticism with *destructive* criticism. If you bring a concern to this type of person, rather than working on the problem in a healthy way, they will instead respond by pointing out all of your faults. They use criticism as a way to shift the focus off them and nothing gets resolved. It is as if they subconsciously feel justified somehow by pointing out all the things that they think you do wrong. Have you ever dealt with someone like this? Maybe you have acted this way to someone else. Whether you have an issue with someone or they have an issue with you, handle it with humility and love. In any conflict no matter who is at fault, being defensive and critical will not solve your problem. Take it to the Lord in prayer, and communicate with an open mind. The Holy Spirit will gently and lovingly bring light to who and what needs to change in the situation. You cannot change your spouse, but you can allow God to work on you; and, you can trust Him also to work on your spouse.

A defensive attitude can lead to a critical spirit. If we resist correction long enough, we will start to become critical in an effort to take the focus off us. In a subtle way, we start pointing out flaws of others in order to keep the attention away from the things that need changing in our own lives. This strategy reveals immaturity. How many times do young children point to the fault of their siblings when they are the one being corrected? Likewise, the spiritually immature are always critically pointing to the mistakes of others to take the focus off themselves. It's always someone else's fault. Self-defense can often lead to the criticism of another. This can be especially true within marriage. Adam pointed to Eve when God questioned him (Genesis 3:9-12). Eve pointed to the devil. Has your spouse ever brought something to your attention, and in defensiveness, you turned the criticism back on your spouse? It is almost as if we somehow feel justified of a wrong if we can point back to the wrongs of others. Nobody wins in this scenario. It only leads to strife and contention. It is a hindrance to unity and to the Lord's anointing.

A synonym for the word "defense" is "justification". Sometimes wrongful accusations are brought against us and we feel the need to defend ourselves. For many years, I would defend myself any time someone brought something against the ministry or me. The Lord convicted me and told me that a man who defends himself will always be average.

THE LORD OUR DEFENSE

We do not need to walk around in our own defense. Jesus is our defense. It is impossible to be defensive and not simultaneously break down your 'rival' in the process. God has not called us to tear each other down. Rather, we are to build one another up in the faith.

> *For I say, through the grace given unto me, to every man that is among you, not to think of himself more highly than he ought to think; but to think soberly, according as God hath dealt to every man the measure of faith* (Romans 12:3).

If someone is criticizing you, you do not have to defend yourself. Take it to the Lord in prayer. Trust Him to be your defense. Always go into prayer about criticism asking God, "Is it me?" If you feel no personal conviction of wrong, let go and let God!

If you are walking uprightly before God, you can trust Him to be your defense. You are not obligated to defend or justify yourself. Trust God to do that. One of His Covenant Names is *Jehovah Maginnenu* meaning *The Lord Our Defense*. There are numerous Scriptures that speak of God as our defender.

> *For the **Lord is our defence** [Maginnenu]; and the Holy One of Israel [Jehovah] is our king* (Psalm 89:18, emphasis added).

> *I will say of the Lord, He is my refuge and my fortress: my God; in him will I trust. Surely he shall deliver thee from the snare of the fowler, and from the noisome pestilence. He*

shall cover thee with his feathers, and under his wings shalt thou trust: his truth shall be thy shield and buckler. Thou shalt not be afraid for the terror by night; nor for the arrow that flieth by day; Nor for the pestilence that walketh in darkness; nor for the destruction that wasteth at noonday. A thousand shall fall at thy side, and ten thousand at thy right hand; but it shall not come nigh thee (Psalm 91:2-7).

He is also called *Jehovah Tsebaoth*, meaning the *Lord of Hosts*. He is the Lord of Battles. A host is a military term meaning battle. The covenant name of God says that He is the *Lord of Battles*. When David faced Goliath, he called God by this name.

*Then said David to the Philistine, Thou comest to me with a sword, and with a spear, and with a shield: but I come to thee in the name of **the LORD of hosts** [Jehovah Tseboath], the God of the armies of Israel, whom thou hast defied. This day will the LORD deliver thee into mine hand; and I will smite thee, and take thine head from thee; and I will give the carcases of the host of the Philistines this day unto the fowls of the air, and to the wild beasts of the earth; that all the earth may know that there is a God in Israel* (1 Samuel 17:45-47, emphasis added).

Jeremiah called God by this name when he was in need of God's defense.

*But, O **Lord of hosts**, that judgest righteously, that triest the reins and the heart, let me see thy vengeance on them:*

for unto thee have I revealed my cause (Jeremiah 11:20, emphasis added).

I love what Moses said to the children of Israel as they were about to cross the Red Sea. They were being pursued by the Egyptians and started to panic. In their frenzy they cried, *"Because there were no graves in Egypt, hast thou taken us away to die in the wilderness? wherefore hast thou dealt thus with us, to carry us forth out of Egypt"* (Exodus 14:11). To this, Moses replied, *"The Lord shall fight for you, and ye shall hold your peace"* (v.14). God did indeed defend them.

> *The Lord is a man of war: the Lord is his name. Pharaoh's chariots and his host hath he cast into the sea: his chosen captains also are drowned in the Red sea* (Exodus 15:3-4).

> *For the Lord your God is he that goeth with you, to fight for you against your enemies, to save you* (Deuteronomy 20:4).

> *Ye shall not fear them: for the Lord your God he shall fight for you* (Deuteronomy 3:22).

> *With him is an arm of flesh; but with us is the Lord our God to help us, and to fight our battles* (2 Chronicles 32:8).

> *I will go before thee, and make the crooked places straight: I will break in pieces the gates of brass, and cut in sunder the bars of iron* (Isaiah 45:2).

It is clear that we do not need to defend ourselves. Our job is to walk uprightly with God. He is our defender and will fight on our behalf. Perhaps the most stunning portrayal of God as our defender is given in Psalm 18. The entire chapter is powerful and I definitely recommend reading it in its entirety. Here are some highlights.

> *The Lord is my rock, and my fortress, and my deliverer; my God, my strength, in whom I will trust; my buckler, and the horn of my salvation, and my high tower. I will call upon the Lord, who is worthy to be praised: so shall I be saved from mine enemies* (Psalm 18:2-3).

> *In my distress I called upon the Lord, and cried unto my God: he heard my voice out of his temple, and my cry came before him, even into his ears. Then the earth shook and trembled; the foundations also of the hills moved and were shaken, because he was wroth. There went up a smoke out of his nostrils, and fire out of his mouth devoured: coals were kindled by it. He bowed the heavens also, and came down: and darkness was under his feet. And he rode upon a cherub, and did fly: yea, he did fly upon the wings of the wind* (v. 6-10).

> *He delivered me from my strong enemy, and from them which hated me: for they were too strong for me. They prevented me in the day of my calamity: but the Lord was my stay. He brought me forth also into a large place; he delivered me, because he delighted in me. The Lord rewarded me according to my righteousness; according to the cleanness of*

my hands hath he recompensed me. For I have kept the ways of the Lord, and have not wickedly departed from my God. For all his judgments were before me, and I did not put away his statutes from me. I was also upright before him, and I kept myself from mine iniquity. Therefore hath the Lord recompensed me according to my righteousness, according to the cleanness of my hands in his eyesight (v. 17-24).

Chapter 7

ENVY

———◆———

E nvy is the feeling of wanting to have what someone else has. It is the painful or resentful awareness of an advantage enjoyed by another, joined with a desire to possess the same advantage. Envy is a feeling of unhappiness over another's good fortune combined with a desire to have the same good fortune. The Bible says that if we are envious, we are carnal:

> *For ye are yet carnal: for whereas there is among you envying,*
> *and strife, and divisions, are ye not carnal, and walk as men?*
> (1 Corinthians 3:3)

Envy is a seed that is rooted in selfishness and pride. I like to think of envy as jealousy on steroids. Jealousy is an anxious feeling that stems from a perceived loss of attention, position or affection. Envy seeks to destroy. It is a stepping-stone to destructive action. In other words, there is a difference between being jealous of what another has and wanting to destroy them because of what they have. Envy gives birth to criticism due to its destructive spirit. As envy increases, it leads to a critical and destructive mindset.

PRIDE GIVES BIRTH TO ENVY

Let us not be desirous of vain glory, provoking one another, envying one another (Galatians 5:26).

*And they that have believing masters, let them not **despise** them, because they are brethren; but rather do them service, because they are faithful and beloved, partakers of the benefit. These things teach and exhort. If any man teach otherwise, and consent not to wholesome words, even the words of our Lord Jesus Christ, and to the doctrine which is according to godliness; He is **proud,** knowing nothing, but doting about questions and **strifes** of words, whereof cometh **envy, strife, railings, evil surmisings, Perverse disputings of men of corrupt minds, and destitute of the truth, supposing that gain is godliness:** from such withdraw thyself* (1 Timothy 6:2-5, emphasis added).

This verse makes it clear that pride gives birth to envy, and leads to quarrels and corruption. It says that if we are proud we know nothing. Selfish pride has the ability to blind us and renders us incapable of seeing truth. The jealous or envious heart is entrapped by a false sense of comparison rooted in pride.

The Bible calls envy vain and fruitless. King Solomon had everything a person could ever want. The book of Ecclesiastes records his thoughts as he searches out the meaning of life. He considers how men work so hard to have more than their neighbor does.

*Again, I considered all travail, and every right work, that
for this a man is envied of his neighbour. This is also vanity
and vexation of spirit* (Ecclesiastes 4:4).

The AMPLIFIED BIBLE puts it this way:

*"Then I saw that all painful effort in labor and all skill in
work comes from man's rivalry with his neighbor. This is also
vanity, a vain striving after the wind and a feeding on it."*

After having done this sort of life experiment in which he withheld
no desire from himself, his conclusion was that being envious of others,
and always striving for more, is meaningless. Solomon comes to this final
realization:

*Let us hear the conclusion of the whole matter: Fear God,
and keep his commandments: for this is the whole duty of
man. For God shall bring every work into judgment, with
every secret thing, whether it be good, or whether it be evil*
(Ecclesiastes 12:13-14).

What we do with our life matters. It is best not to waste time being
envious and critical of what other people have. What we should be concerned about is pleasing God. This life is temporary, but the next is eternal.
Just as Solomon pointed out, it would be a waste of our time here to chase
after riches or fame. We cannot take any of it with us into eternity. Instead,
we should follow after righteousness.

But godliness with contentment is great gain. For we brought nothing into this world, and it is certain we can carry nothing out. And having food and raiment let us be therewith content. But they that will be rich fall into temptation and a snare, and into many foolish and hurtful lusts, which drown men in destruction and perdition. For the love of money is the root of all evil: which while some coveted after, they have erred from the faith, and pierced themselves through with many sorrows. But thou, O man of God, flee these things; and follow after righteousness, godliness, faith, love, patience, meekness (1 Timothy 6:6-11).

Envy is never of God. Let me explain. We have already discussed that God is no respecter of persons. He loves everyone the same and everyone has equal access to His promises by faith. We are all sinners and we all need Jesus. Because Jesus died for all mankind, anyone who is willing to repent and call on Him will be saved. Anyone who has been saved has become a co-heir with Christ and has the same ability to petition God for anything they need.

If a person is envious, it means that they either do not know God or they do not understand that they have the same access to God as anyone else. When we realize that God will meet all of our needs, envy becomes unnecessary.

If envy exist in us, it is coming from our flesh and not our spirit. Christians need to realize the danger of allowing envy to remain in their hearts so that they may deal with it quickly. It will not produce good fruit, nor will it glorify God. Ultimately, envy will lead to pain. Because envy stems from pride and selfishness, we must be diligent about repentance if we are to escape the trap where it will lead.

Joseph was a man who had been given dreams by God. His brothers became envious of him as he told them about his dreams. They were also envious of his favor with their father Jacob.

> *Now Israel [Jacob] loved Joseph more than all his children,*
> *because he was the son of his old age: and he made him a*
> *coat of many colours. And when his brethren saw that their*
> *father loved him more than all his brethren, they hated him,*
> *and could not speak peaceably unto him* (Genesis 37:3-4).

Joseph's brothers allowed their envy to take root and grow. The more Joseph revealed his dreams, the more they grew to resent him. Their criticism is evident in the way they spoke to him.

> *And his brethren said to him, Shalt thou indeed reign over*
> *us? or shalt thou indeed have dominion over us? And they*
> *hated him yet the more for his dreams, and for his words.*
> *And he dreamed yet another dream, and told it his brethren...*
> *And his brethren envied him; but his father observed the*
> *saying* (v. 9, 11).

Finally, the brothers could not take it anymore. Their envy drove them to a wicked and terrible decision. First, they considered killing him. Then they came up with a different plot. They decided to sell him into slavery and to tell his father some evil beast killed him. These siblings were driven to almost murder their own brother! This story illustrates the evil power of envy! It did not happen overnight. It began as a seed of jealousy and grew into an ungodly and terrible decision of envy.

Ultimately, Joseph's brothers were humbled. Their jealousy caused them to end up losing all of their wealth and resources. In the end, they would have to go to Joseph begging for his help. God favored Joseph because his heart was upright. He did end up reigning over his brothers, as his dreams originally prophesied. He used his position to show mercy instead of judgment.

ENVY: THE CRITIC'S GREATER ISSUE

Another rather direct example of how envy can lead to criticism is found in Acts 13.

Now when the congregation was broken up, many of the Jews and religious proselytes [devout converts] *followed Paul and Barnabas: who, speaking to them, persuaded them to continue in the grace of God. And the next sabbath day came almost the whole city together to hear the word of God. But when the Jews saw the multitudes, they were filled with envy,* ***and spake against those things which were spoken by Paul, contradicting and blaspheming.*** *Then Paul and Barnabas waxed bold, and said, It was necessary that the word of God should first have been spoken to you: but seeing ye put it from you, and judge yourselves unworthy of everlasting life, lo, we turn to the Gentiles* (Acts 13:43-46, emphasis added).

Envy makes people do crazy things. It made even the most devout religious Jews speak against the doctrine they were so devoted to. Beforehand, these Jews had followed Paul and Barnabas. However, when they saw that the two men were speaking the Word of God to the multitudes of Gentiles, they suddenly became critical of them. Their envy led them to begin to 'stir up' the influential people of the city. They began to persecute Paul and Barnabas and used criticism to 'get people on their side.'

I have witnessed this mindset in action first-hand, having dealt with people who are extremely critical of me and of the ministry that God has placed me in. Once, during a teaching on "stewardship", I was opposed by a brother who challenged me to say that he was a "son" of God—not a steward. I realized that his criticism had nothing to do with the term "steward" but everything to do with his opposition to me, the ministry, and the content of the message that was preached. I agree; we are "sons" of God. We are His children through faith in Christ. That does not negate our being stewards. My children have to learn management. Their success or failure in that does not determine if they are my children; but it will determine what I am able to give them oversight of and their success in managing it.

There will always be someone waiting in the wings to offer their voice of criticism. However, the topic of debate might not be the root of the issue. In most cases, the critic has a greater issue—envy. I have stated for years that your critics are likely individuals who are jealous of you.

We have to learn how to address envy when it is directed at us. We must also remain sensitive to God's will and word, being careful not to allow envy to manifest in our own hearts. If you are tempted with envy, do not let it get the best of you. You have the Holy Spirit living inside and He will help you to rid yourself of it.

> *From the end of the earth will I cry unto thee, when my heart is overwhelmed: lead me to the rock that is higher than I* (Psalm 61:2).

Like as a father pitieth his children, so the Lord pitieth them that fear him. For he knoweth our frame; he remembereth that we are dust (Psalm 103:13-14).

Neither murmur [despondently complain] *ye, as some of them also murmured, and were destroyed of the destroyer. Wherefore let him that thinketh he standeth take heed lest he fall. There hath no temptation taken you but such as is common to man: but God is faithful, who will not suffer you to be tempted above that ye are able; but will with the temptation also make a way to escape, that ye may be able to bear it* (1 Corinthians 10:10, 12-13).

Thou therefore endure hardness, as a good soldier of Jesus Christ. No man that warreth entangleth himself with the affairs of this life; that he may please him who hath chosen him to be a soldier (2 Timothy 2:3-4).

Humble yourselves therefore under the mighty hand of God, that he may exalt you in due time: Casting all your care upon him; for he careth for you. Be sober, be vigilant; because your adversary the devil, as a roaring lion, walketh about, seeking whom he may devour: Whom resist stedfast in the faith, knowing that the same afflictions are accomplished in your brethren that are in the world. But the God of all grace, who hath called us unto his eternal glory by Christ Jesus, after that ye have suffered a while, make you perfect, stablish, strengthen, settle you (1 Peter 5:6-10).

Chapter 8

CRITIC OR COUNSELOR?

We have looked at criticism through the acrostic of P.R.I.D.E and how it can manifest through Preference, Resentment, Inferiority, Defensiveness, and Envy. At this point, you might be wondering if there is ever a time or context in which it is appropriate to be critical. As I stated in Chapter 2, there are times we must use "sound judgment." There are certainly times that merit righteous critique. In those instances, we must learn how to remain submitted to God's Spirit. It is important to be influenced by His grace, to stay true to His Word, and above all—to be rooted in love.

According to the 1828 Webster's Dictionary, the word *critical* means:

1. Relating to criticism; nicely exact; as a critical dissertation on Homer.

2. Having the skill or power nicely to distinguish beauties from blemishes; a critical judge; a critical auditor; a critical ear; critical taste.

3. Making nice distinctions; accurate; as critical rules.

4. Capable of judging with accuracy; discerning beauties and faults; nicely judicious in matters of literature and the fine arts; as, Virgil was a critical poet.

5. Capable of judging with accuracy; conforming to exact rules of propriety; exact; particular; as, to be critical in rites and ceremonies, or in the selection of books.

6. Inclined to find fault, or to judge with severity.

According to the definition above, one who is critical should know what they are doing. How else could someone always 'judge with accuracy' and 'make accurate distinctions'? One would pretty much have to be perfect in order to fit the criteria listed above. God is the only one who is perfect and capable of judging rightly in every situation. He has all knowledge and can see things we cannot see. Thankfully, He has given us His standards of judgment in His Word. The Bible tells us that it is righteous and profitable for teaching, for reproof, for correction, and for training in righteousness (2 Timothy 3:16). It gives us wisdom and direction for life. Therefore, instead of making our own judgments on any issue – for an example, forgiveness–we can instead use His standard of judgment. That way we can know that we are discerning rightly. Think of His word as a standard for counsel.

Considering this begs the question, are you a critic or counselor? There is certainly a difference between the two. As I mentioned earlier, there are times that merit righteous critique. However, critique is only righteous if it is based on God's Word. If we are not making distinctions and judgments based on the Word of God as our counsel, then our criticism is not righteous, it is carnal. Think about how many times the Bible uses the word "counsel." Here are a few of them:

Counsel is mine, and sound wisdom: I am understanding;
I have strength (Proverbs 8:14).

Without counsel purposes are disappointed: but in the mul-
titude of   counsellors they are established. The fear of
the Lord is the instruction of wisdom; and before honour is
humility (Proverbs 15:22, 33).

I will bless the Lord, who hath given me counsel
(Proverbs 16:7).

There are many devices in a man's heart; nevertheless the
counsel of the Lord, that shall stand (Proverbs 19:21).

The counsel of the Lord standeth for ever, the thoughts of his
heart to all generations (Psalms 33:11).

You see, as believers we have the Spirit of the Lord living in us. Because of this, we can go to the Lord with anything and He can use His Word to instruct us. Consider what God said to Ezekiel, *"And I will put my spirit within you, and cause you to walk in my statutes, and ye shall keep my judgments, and do them"* (Ezekiel 36:27). That same promise applies to all believers. Psalm 32 says, *"I will instruct thee and teach thee in the way which thou shalt go: I will guide thee with mine eye"* (v. 8). We can rest assured that if we live according to God's instruction, we have taken the right path.

If we counsel according to His Word, our counsel is righteous. The Lord will always make good on His Word!

Let's talk about what differentiates a critic and a counselor. Critics and counselors can be discerned by their righteous/unrighteous characteristics. A critic tells everyone your business; a counselor will only talk to you. Counsel is invited while criticism is forced upon you. A critic has his or her own interests at heart. A counselor has your best interest in mind. Since criticism is part of the enemy's strategy to divide the body of Christ, we need to know how to discern between a critic and a counselor, and how to deal with each. I do believe there are occasions where the critic will disguise themselves as a counselor. I have witnessed the "critic" show up as a "counselor" while adding the weight of "the Spirit told me to tell you..." Their motive along with the agreement or disagreement in your heart will bring exposure. The fruit of the Spirit is peace and it will always lead us and guard our heart.

Christians are called to be counselors. We need to know how to offer help and Biblical support in the right way, without tearing others down. We also need to know the way to respond to a destructive and critical spirit in a way that honors God. The only way to conquer criticism is to operate in the spirit of meekness. As Christians, we speak the truth in love.

> *Let nothing be done through strife or vainglory; but in lowliness of mind let each esteem other better than themselves* (Philippians 2:3).

Ungodly criticism tears down. Godly counsel builds up. Isaiah 10:27 declares that the anointing of the Spirit will remove our burdens and destroy yokes. Isaiah 11:2 lists "counsel" as an anointing. True godly counsel, authored by a sensitivity to the Spirit of God, will remove burdens and destroy yokes! I thank God for those who have counseled me through the years.

Sadly, there are many who have no desire to counsel because their intentions are not good. They would rather operate through criticism and condemnation because they are more concerned with serving their selfish intentions. As Christians, our objective should be to edify not destroy.

MOTIVATED BY ANGER?

An angry man stirreth up strife, and a furious man aboundeth in transgression (Proverbs 29:22).

Being able to give and receive Biblical counsel is the right of every Christian. We may not all have reached the same level of maturity, but as ambassadors of Christ, our lives should reflect Him. Anger is a major obstacle to a life of godliness. Think about yourself for a moment. Are you the type of person people can talk to? How do you respond to correction? Do you get angry easily? How do you act when your temper flares? These are hard questions to ask, but they are worth addressing. Anger is a resounding theme in the Bible. It is a human emotion that will happen to everyone at some point. The key is knowing what to do with anger. Let us look at some of the things the Bible says about anger.

Be ye angry, and sin not: let not the sun go down upon your wrath: Neither give place to the devil (Ephesians 4:26-27).

It is not wrong to feel angry, but it is wrong to hold on to or harbor it. Anger needs to be addressed swiftly or it can lead you into sin. This verse says that when we hold on to anger we are giving the devil a foothold. It is like opening a door that will allow the enemy to influence your life and thoughts. Do not allow it! Instead, pray and seek God. Be resolved to address the source of your anger in a Godly way and then let it go!

> *Let no corrupt communication proceed out of your mouth, but that which is good to the use of edifying, that it may minister grace unto the hearers. And grieve not the holy Spirit of God, whereby ye are sealed unto the day of redemption. Let all bitterness, and wrath, and anger, and clamour, and evil speaking, be put away from you, with all malice: And be ye kind one to another, tenderhearted, forgiving one another, even as God for Christ's sake hath forgiven you* (Ephesians 4:29-32).

Don't let your anger cause you to act in an ungodly way. Again, it is not wrong to feel angry; but it is wrong to yell or degrade others because of it. '*Corrupt communication*' can be a number of things. It can come out in the form of hostility, gossip, condescension, sarcasm, bitterness, or a general lack of care. If you have a temper problem, you need to seek God for strength in that area and allow Him to renew your mind. When you feel your temper flare, ask yourself, "Is what I am about to say kind and can it be used to edify? Would Jesus be pleased with what I am about to say?" If you are in an angry moment and do not feel like you can say something that reflects God's tender forgiveness, it might be good to take a few moments by yourself and pray. Be real with God about whatever is making you angry and ask for His help. I find it beneficial to go to God privately and share with Him my feelings. It is amazing the difference I feel once I have openly shared my heart with Him. He will always give you the grace you need to move forward in a way that reflects Him.

> *Wherefore, my beloved brethren, let every man be swift to hear, slow to speak, slow to wrath: For the wrath of man worketh not the righteousness of God* (James 1:19-20).

God requires that we learn patience. The Amplified version phrases it like this, "*Understand this, my beloved brethren. Let every man be quick to hear [a ready listener], slow to speak, slow to take offense and to get angry. For man's anger does not promote the righteousness God [wishes and requires].*" A person who allows himself to act angry and temperamental needs to learn patience. That type of behavior does not reflect the kind of righteousness God requires of His children. This is a big deal to God. He goes so far as to say, "*If any man among you seem to be religious, and bridleth not his tongue, but deceiveth his own heart, this man's religion is vain*" (James 1:26). Simply put, a person may feel that he is living a godly life, but if he cannot control his temper, he is deceiving himself.

> *Be not hasty in thy spirit to be angry: for anger resteth in the bosom of fools* (Ecclesiastes 7:9).

> *The discretion of a man deferreth his anger; and it is his glory to pass over a transgression* (Proverbs 19:11).

> *My brethren, count it all joy when ye fall into divers temptations; Knowing this, that the trying of your faith worketh patience. But let patience have her perfect work, that ye may be perfect and entire, wanting nothing. If any of you lack wisdom, let him ask of God, that giveth to all men liberally, and upbraideth not; and it shall be given him* (James 1:2-5).

The verses above make it clear that the Bible equates patience with wisdom. Therefore, a person who is easily angered lacks patience and wisdom. The Bible calls it foolish to be hasty in anger. It is godly wisdom in a person that produces patience. The verse above says that we should actually be glad when our patience is tried because it is an opportunity to learn and to receive God's strength to change.

If you find that you have a quick temper and that you need help, ask God to restore and heal you. He will give you the grace you need to learn patience, thereby increasing your wisdom. Use every instance that you are angry as an opportunity to work at building your patience. Master it. Do not let it master you.

> *He that is slow to wrath is of great understanding: but he that is hasty of spirit exalteth folly. Wisdom resteth in the heart of him that hath understanding: but that which is in the midst of fools is made known* (Proverbs 14:29, 33).

> *He that is slow to anger is better than the mighty; and he that ruleth his spirit than he that taketh a city. The lot is cast into the lap; but the whole disposing thereof is of the Lord* (Proverbs 16:32-33).

Anger holds a person back. A person who is hasty in anger shows a lack of discipline. An angry, undisciplined person cannot be trusted with important assignments from God because they will not see the situation clearly; and they will not have the discipline to carry out the Lord's instruction – especially in the face of opposition. They will instead act out of anger. Because the anger of man does not produce the righteousness of God, how can one expect to carry out God's righteous decrees when they are angry?

We have already noted the fact that anger causes us to be deceived. I looked up the word 'disposing' from the verse above in Strong's Exhaustive Concordance of the Bible. It refers to *the act of making a judgment, deciding a case, making of a decision, or the right to execute judgment.* That right belongs to God. We all get angry at times. Things do not always go the way we want. Even in those instances, we have not been given the right to act out in anger. We may be the ones in the 'lot' or situation, but the act of executing judgment belongs to the Lord. Our job is to take issues to God in prayer, and to show forgiveness. A quick-tempered person will not do this. They will just act in the moment out of anger.

One who shows the discipline to control his anger can be trusted by God to carry out his instructions. It makes sense that the Bible would connect patience with wisdom. God can trust a patient and disciplined person to control his emotions and obey the commandments He has given. Remember Moses? His anger caused him to be left out of entering the Promised Land. It could be that God was telling us there is no place for anger in the Promised Land.

A person with an angry spirit will not give correct Biblical counsel because they are deceived and motivated by emotion. Anger causes us to have a skewed perception of reality. It is the patience and compassion of Jesus that God wants us to represent. Before offering guidance, counsel or correction, be sure that you have rid yourself of anger. This can be especially relevant when addressing your children. Do not ever allow the disciplining of your children to be motivated by anger. Search your heart for anger and repent of it. It is a decision you will not regret.

*Finally, be ye all of one mind, having compassion one
of another, love as brethren, be pitiful, be courteous:
Not rendering evil for evil, or railing for railing: but
contrariwise blessing; knowing that ye are thereunto
called, that ye should inherit a blessing. For he that
will love life, and see good days, let him refrain his
tongue from evil, and his lips that they speak no guile:
Let him eschew evil, and do good; let him seek peace,
and ensue it. For the eyes of the Lord are over the
righteous, and his ears are open unto their prayers:
but the face of the Lord is against them that do evil.
And who is he that will harm you, if ye be followers of
that which is good? But and if ye suffer for righteousness' sake, happy are ye: and be not afraid of their
terror, neither be troubled; But sanctify the Lord God
in your hearts: and be ready always to give an answer
to every man that asketh you a reason of the hope
that is in you with meekness and fear: Having a good
conscience; that, whereas they speak evil of you, as
of evildoers, they may be ashamed that falsely accuse
your good conversation in Christ* (1 Peter 3:8-16).

THE CONTROLLING CRITIC

*Then went the Pharisees, and took counsel how they might
entangle him in his talk. And they sent out unto him their
disciples with the Herodians, saying, Master, we know that
thou art true, and teachest the way of God in truth, neither
carest thou for any man: for thou regardest not the person*

of men. Tell us therefore, What thinkest thou? Is it lawful to give tribute unto Caesar, or not? (Matthew 22:15-17).

Anger can also drive a person to become controlling. Intimidation, domination, and manipulation are all means in which one person uses to control another person. These things are forms of witchcraft or mind-control. Intimidation says, "I will scare you into submission." Domination says, "I will make you submit." However, manipulation is more subtle. It is to deceive, trick, play, or con the mind into submission. I am convinced that criticism is a form of manipulation. In other words, there will be some that will use criticism simply to control you.

In the verse quoted above, we see the Pharisees acknowledged that Jesus regarded *"not the person of men"* (Matthew 22:16). This meant they knew he was not under the control of men. However, this did not stop them from wanting to control Jesus. They were angered with His teachings and had to come up with a manipulative way to control Jesus. Their method was criticism. Their attempts did not work, but we can learn from their tactics. When your enemies cannot find any other way to control you, they will criticize you!

The religious authorities in Jesus' day were in constant criticism. Perhaps when we see how much Jesus was criticized, we will walk free of the controlling criticism of others. He was criticized for who He ate with (Matthew 9:1); for His disciples' "unlawful" actions on the Sabbath (Matthew 12:2); for not providing a sign that met the expectations of His critics (Matthew 12:38; 16:1); for His disciples eating without washing their hands (Mark 7:1-2); and for allowing a sinful woman to anoint His feet in gratitude of forgiveness (Luke 7:36-39).

The Bible teaches us that these self-righteous critics literally sought to find fault, entangle, and catch Him in His words (Mark 7:2, Matthew

22:15, Mark 12:13). In one occasion, Jesus was invited into their home. Even as their guest, He was called a "sinner" (Luke 7:36-39). Sometimes people will invite you into their presence only for the sake of finding evidence for criticism. They hope to entangle you in your words. This type of criticism is motivated by anger and used for the purpose of control.

> *The thief cometh not, but for to steal, and to kill, and to destroy: I am come that they might have life, and that they might have it more abundantly* (John 10:10).

Believers, let us not be found using the tactics of the enemy! I believe that the devil himself uses criticism to control us. He is constantly using the methods of guilt and condemnation to drive us from the saving and delivering grace of Jesus. He loves to remind us of our shortcomings. He also influences us to point out the short-comings of others. He wants to use us as pawns for his strategies. A *pawn* is someone who is used or manipulated to further another person's purposes [dictionary.com]. We must not allow the enemy to use us to advance his plan. Fear, guilt, condemnation, criticism, manipulation, and anger are all part of his strategy to kill, steal and destroy (John 10:10). The weapons may be formed, however, in Jesus' Name, and according to Isaiah 54:17, they will not prosper!

Chapter 9

DESTRUCTIVE CRITICISM

A nger is a seed that can lead to destructive criticism. When we allow anger to remain in us, it produces a harvest of unholy and ungodly fruit. Destructive criticism is a painful force that isolates. It can cause serious damage and we must be careful to avoid being used as a vessel for it. As I stated in the previous chapter, the enemy wants to use us as pawns to his agenda—an agenda "to kill, steal and destroy" (John 10:10, emphasis added). Destructive criticism is a means to his objective. We must be on guard!

Destructive criticism manifests in many ways. It can be given or received. If you have ever been in an intense argument with your spouse, it is likely you have thought to leave. I am not saying you should leave. When you leave, you practice or rehearse divorce. My point is that you get the feelings of wanting to leave because you are withdrawing away from the criticism you are receiving. You might be on the giving end of that criticism. It is likely that you were motivated by hurt that turned into anger. This is why it is so important to quickly deal with issues, especially anger. If they are not addressed, they lead to more problems.

The devil loves to isolate. When we dish out destructive criticism, we lend him a hand in isolation. 1 Kings 18 and 19 tell the story of Elijah.

He was a prophet of God who challenged all the false prophets of Baal to a showdown and won! Right after this amazing victory, where he had just called down fire from heaven, he gets word that Jezebel was after him. She sends a report to Elijah telling him that she would kill him within 24 hours. Elijah decides to run and hide in a cave. He allowed one critic to send him into isolation, after which he starts to feel pitiful. He starts telling God, "*I'm the only prophet that remains.*" The reality wasn't as bad as it was in Elijah's mind. Because the enemy was able to isolate him, the situation seemed much worse than it actually was. It is a common tactic of the enemy to isolate. Do not allow yourself to be the tool he uses to isolate others. Refuse to be the bearer of destructive criticism.

We must be so careful how we use our words. Proverbs 18:21 says that death and life are in the power of the tongue. Ask yourself, "Do I want to give death or do I want to give life?" Your words reflect what is in your heart. They can build up or tear down those who receive them. Your intent may be good. You may think your intent is justified. It is important to remember that the impact your words have on others may outweigh your intentions. People will not always remember what was said; but they *will* remember how you made them feel. I have learned this the hard way. God expects us to be mindful of the way we speak to others and the impact we are making on the people around us. If there is anything more powerful than our words, it is the motive behind them. If your motive is not pure (at the time), hold your words of criticism.

DESTRUCTIVE CRITICISM IS SELFISH

And I heard a loud voice saying in heaven, Now is come salvation, and strength, and the kingdom of our God, and the power of his Christ: for the accuser of our brethren is cast

down, which accused them before our God day and night
(Revelation 12:10).

The world "devil" means slanderer. When we think higher of ourselves than we ought to, we lift ourselves up in pride. This is exactly what Satan was doing when he was cast out of heaven. Be careful that you do not allow yourself to become a vessel that is used by the enemy to bring poison and to injure people. If we name the Name of Jesus, we should not be walking around in a critical spirit driving people away from God.

Honestly assess the way you deal with people when you are angry. If you are unwilling to do this, it means that you are content to allow your anger to persist. It means you are choosing yourself and your own emotions over God's divine decree. Destructive criticism is not of God. It comes from a fleshly, selfish part of us. Our words, particularly words meant to correct, should be meek and full of love.

> *The meek also shall increase their joy in the Lord, and the poor among men shall rejoice in the Holy One of Israel. For the terrible one is brought to nought, and the scorner is consumed, and all that watch for iniquity are cut off: That make a man an offender for a word, and lay a snare for him that reproveth in the gate, and turn aside the just for a thing of nought* (Isaiah 29:19-21).

As Christians—and especially as the Church—we must be sensitive to not set ourselves in a seat of judgment because we will isolate the unbeliever. Destructive criticism and a judgmental spirit will drive those who need Jesus away from Him. As ambassadors of Christ, we have to give others the grace to grow. Our words need to draw them into fellowship with God—not drive them away. Likewise, we should apply this to our relationships and certainly our marriages. Do you words draw your loved one closer or drive them away?

Remember, criticism always points to the problem. Counselors point to the solution. Criticism is negative and unhealthy. It destroys relationships. It is used to manipulate and control people. It is ungodly. It will form a wedge in marriages. Instead, we should speak the truth in love (Ephesians 4:15). By doing so, we are respecting the command God gave us.

CRITICISM DISRESPECTS THE DIVINE ORDER OF GOD

We serve a God of order. He gave us His Word so that we would know the right way to deal with each other, and so that we could live a joyful and abundant life. God's Word gives us order in life so that we can prosper. It is a reflection of His heart and His ways. Destructive criticism directly defies the Word of God. It disrespects the order and method in which He has told us to operate.

Consider this illustration. Say you and your wife have an argument. You would not go to your children and criticize their mom. That is dishonorable. If you have an issue with your spouse, you take it to her directly. In the same way, God has asked us to come to Him with our problems and to show love to the ones we feel are causing them. Remember, your wife is also a child of God. She is an imperfect human being, just as you are. You cannot change her, and your critical spirit will only serve to isolate her. Only God can influence the heart of His children to bring about true and lasting change. When we take our criticism to Him in prayer, it shows that we are respecting Him as the righteous judge. It means that we are allowing Him to decide who is right and who needs to be changed, and we are allowing Him to execute that decision as He sees fit. By doing this, it shows we are honoring God as our Sovereign and loving Father. It is showing Him the respect He deserves.

> *And Miriam and Aaron spake against Moses because of the Ethiopian woman whom he had married: for he had married an Ethiopian woman. And they said, Hath the Lord indeed spoken only by Moses? hath he not spoken also by us? And the Lord heard it* (Number 12:1-2).

Here is an instance in which Moses' brother and sister became critical of him. They spoke against him for having married an Ethiopian woman. What is interesting is that it was only in their anger that they started to question if Moses was the only one God could speak through. I cannot help but wonder were they jealous of him being used as God's prophet, and therefore looking to criticize whatever they could find (who he chose to marry)? Or, were they indeed critical of his marital preference, and therefore ready to discount him as a prophet? Regardless of the answer, God was not pleased! If you read the rest of the story you will see where God validated and further endorsed Moses as his prophet and rebuked Aaron and Miriam. Miriam became leprous and was shut out of the camp for seven days before she was healed and restored!

Miriam had taken it upon herself, along with Aaron, to criticize Moses and to demean the call of God on his life. They disrespected the divine order of God. I have witnessed this many times. I have seen pastors and ministers attacked due to some personal preference. I have personally been attacked many times either for the color of my skin or because I pastor an integrated church. There is an audacity present when we take it upon ourselves to judge others. I encourage you to be cautious. The word says that when Miriam and Aaron spake against Moses, *"...the Lord heard it"* (Numbers 12:2).

If you feel that you are on the receiving end of unfair and unjust criticism, remember Moses, who was meek, despite his critics. *"Now the man Moses was very meek, above all the men which were upon the face of the earth"* (v. 3). Just as Moses did, let the Lord be your defense. Let the Lord fight your battles! He has a way of correcting the critics.

LET THY WORDS BE FEW

There is a powerful verse in the Book of Ecclesiastes that can certainly be applied to criticism. Notice:

> *Be not rash with thy mouth, and let not thine heart be hasty*
> *to utter any thing before God: for God is in heaven, and thou*
> *upon earth: therefore let thy words be few* (Ecclesiastes 5:2).

There are a few things we can pull from this verse and apply to our lives. First, we should be slow to speak— *"Be not rash with thy mouth."* Second, do not assume you have the right to speak before or for God— *"for God is in heaven, and thou upon earth."* He sees and understands things we could never comprehend or discern. I am cautious of those who constantly claim to be speaking on behalf of the Holy Spirit. Finally, *"let thy words be few."* I believe one of the greatest compliments a person could ever give you is to have someone say that they have never heard you speak a negative word about anyone else.

Remember what Jesus said about giving (and this applies to everything that you give—including criticism and judgment), *"Give, and it shall be given unto you; good measure, pressed down, and shaken together, and running over, shall men give into your bosom. For with the same measure that ye mete withal it shall be measured to you again"* (Luke 6:38). What you give is what you will get. For the same measure you mete, it shall be measured unto you again. What kind of measuring tool will you use when you judge? The same measurement you use will be returned to you in good measure, pressed down, shaken together and running over. No wonder the Bible says, *"let thy words be few."*

MAKING ASSESSMENTS

It is easy to find flaws in others. We have no trouble holding other people to the highest of standards. It is harder to apply the same standards to our own lives. We are prone to go easier on ourselves and to overlook our own actions. Romans 2:1, *"Therefore thou art inexcusable, O man, whosoever thou art that judgest: for wherein thou judgest another, thou condemnest thyself; for thou that judgest doest the same things."* Humility is key to a successful life. When you get the urge to be critical of someone else, stop and check your own heart.

King David had committed a sin with Bathsheba, who was married to someone else. She ends up having David's child. To cover the whole thing up, David had her husband—one of his own friends—murdered. Nathan, a prophet of God, approaches him wisely, knowing that his approach would affect the way David received his criticism. Nathan told David a story about two men, one rich and one poor. The rich man had plenty of resources, and the poor man had only one little lamb to his name. Nathan tells David how the rich man did something evil. When a traveler came through town, the rich man, though he had plenty of lambs in his flock, took the poor man's one and only lamb and dressed it for a meal. David hears this story and responds, *"as the Lord liveth, the man that has done this thing shall surely die,"* Nathan says, *"thou art the man."* When it was someone else, David was ready to kill him. However, he realizes he had done the same type of evil. It was harder to see to judge himself righteously knowing what he had done.

All of our relationships need to be approached in the spirit of humility.

This is especially true of marriage. In marriage, you have to choose your conflicts that you an engage in with wisdom. Do not be critical of everything. Put yourself in your spouse's shoes. You may not have had to carpool kids all day so do not get mad if the car is a little dirty. If you start criticizing everything your spouse is doing, everything that is wrong in the house, or everything that is not right, you will find yourself only criticizing all the time. *"It is better to dwell in a corner of the housetop, than with a brawling woman in a wide house."* (Proverbs 21:9). The word "brawling" means contentious, quarrelsome or debating. The Bible here states the man is better off on a small roof than in a large house where there is criticism and strife. This certainly does not discount that there are men (husbands) who can be equally as critical. The point I am making is to not allow your home to become a place of bitterness and strife. Who wants to abide in such an atmosphere? Our homes should be havens of peace, not dens of criticism.

There is always something to be critical about because that is life and things happen. The key is to choose with measure. Ask yourself, "What measure do I want to mete with my criticism?" Don't make your home a house of criticism. Keep in mind that the things you say will judge you.

For he shall have judgment without mercy, that hath shewed no mercy; and mercy rejoiceth against judgment (James 2:13).

This verse echoes the message of Jesus. What you sow is what you will reap. Do you want mercy when you need it? Then give mercy when someone else needs it. This verse also teaches us that mercy will prevail over judgment! That is something we can all thank God for—that His mercy has prevailed over His judgment. If only we Christians would live that out as it relates to others.

I discussed this topic one Monday morning in our weekly staff meeting. One of my staff members voiced her solution for when she felt tempted to become critical of anyone. She informed our staff that when she finds herself being critical, she chooses to make a stronger connection with that person. She noted that, more often than not, when we meet the heart of a person and hear their 'back story', we change our critical view and become more understanding. It is easier to be sensitive when you understand where someone is coming from or what he or she are going through. Are you being critical towards someone? Make a decision today to make a greater connection with them. If that is not something you are willing to do, then end the criticism—it is not working to draw that life closer to God.

I had a man approach me who had been visiting our church. He told me how he had never heard preaching like he was getting; but then alluded to his dislike of my not standing out in the foyer before and after services on Sunday. He shared how his previous pastor would greet everyone in the foyer after Sunday service. I asked him how many times his previous pastor preached on Sunday. He said once, if that. I then shared how I preached three services back-to-back-to-back. I informed him that on Wednesdays, where I minister once, I hang out in the foyer after services to visit with the people. However, on Sunday there's no way my voice would hold up to meet and greet thousands of people and preach three times. Once he heard my heart, he completely understood. Unfortunately, there are some driven by a critical spirit, that like to plant thoughts of judgment without ever seeking to assess a situation or try to understand it. I was thankful for the conversation I had with this brother. It is amazing how our criticism towards someone can change once we connect with them and see their heart.

Judgment drives. Mercy draws. We are drawn to God because of His goodness and mercy (Romans 2:4). For instance, you do not want to be so critical of your husband or wife that the first time another man or woman says something positive to them, it draws them away from you. There is too much water in the world for anyone to leave home thirsty. Meaning, there are too many opportunities for someone to be tempted to look elsewhere to get their needs for love and acceptance met. The enemy loves to assault our minds with lies and twisted truths. Why even give him the opportunity to whisper lies to your spouse? For example, he might plant the thought, "Your coworker would treat you better than your spouse. She really understands you." Obviously that is an ungodly thought that the enemy might use as a stepping stone towards adultery. It's not pretty and our enemy doesn't play nice. It's why the Bible warns us to be vigilant. Satan is actively looking for someone to devour (1 Peter 5:8).

The point is that it is our first instinct is to get away from the source of judgment and criticism towards us. We want to separate ourselves from it. Do not be the tool of the enemy that drives your spouse away because you are so critical of them. I am not at all condoning the idea of any form of infidelity. I am merely trying to unveil what might be the plot of the enemy. If you took the time you spend in conversation with your spouse and cut it up like you would a piece of pie, how much of the pie (time) is spent being critical or complaining? There is no way to have a healthy marriage when the bulk of the time is spent dealing with criticism. Perhaps if we spent more time complimenting and building one another up, the things we might otherwise be critical of would begin to resolve themselves. I would much rather minister to my wife's needs out of the desire of my heart than the complaint of her criticism. There is no way to have a healthy relationship when it is blanketed by criticism. We are far more inclined to respond positively to encouragement than we are complaint. In many cases, the critical spouse is still not satisfied with modified behavior. There new complaint is, "I had to criticize you to get you to change." Don't let criticism become a negative force in your home or marriage driving your loved one away.

I have seen this same principal manifest in the church. Has the Body of Christ been influenced by bad religion and self-righteousness? Have believers become so hard, condemning and judgmental that we are driving souls deeper into the world? Jesus came not into the world to condemn it, but to save it! (John 3:17). I have found that making the standard of God's Word relevant to the hearer will draw the lost to salvation and sanctification, whereas pointing the finger of condemnation and judgment only drives away the lost from a grace that could have saved them!

Chapter 10

CONSTRUCTIVE CRITICISM

---❖---

Open rebuke is better than secret love. Faithful are the wounds of a friend; but the kisses of an enemy are deceitful. The full soul loatheth an honeycomb; but to the hungry soul every bitter thing is sweet (Proverbs 27:5-7).

I believe the defining aspect of godly, constructive counsel or critique is love. If you are not covering an issue in love, it is not constructive. There are many ideas floating around in the world about what love is and what love looks like. We may have adopted some wrong ideas about love without even realizing it. The Bible gives us the true definition of what love looks like. If you want to be sure that you are acting in love, do the Biblical love test.

Charity (love) suffereth long, and is kind; charity envieth not; charity vaunteth not itself, is not puffed up, Doth not behave itself unseemly, seeketh not her own, is not easily provoked, thinketh no evil; Rejoiceth not in iniquity, but rejoiceth in the truth; Beareth all things, believeth all things, hopeth all things, endureth all things (1 Corinthians 13:4-7).

Take your actions and weigh them against this verse. Below is a list of questions to ask yourself that will help you determine if you are operating in love.

- Am I being patient?
- Are my words/actions kind?
- Is there any envy in my heart that may be motivating me?
- Am I acting in anger?
- Am I seeking only to prove my point and get my own needs met?
- Do I have all the facts, or am I assuming the worst?
- Am I giving the person I am angry at the benefit of the doubt?
- Am I genuinely listening or am I just biting my tongue and thinking about what I want to say?
- Am I allowing room for grace and mercy?
- Am I problem minded or solution minded?
- Am I operating in hope?
- Is my approach pleasing to Jesus?
- Are my words gentle and meek?
- If I were in the other person's shoes, am I dealing with them the way I would want to be dealt with?

We do not have to sacrifice truth in order to meet any of the questions listed above. Operating in love does not mean denying our feelings. It means we are expressing them in a way that is acceptable and pleasing to God.

For all the law is fulfilled in one word, even in this; Thou shalt love thy neighbour as thyself. But if ye bite and devour one another, take heed that ye be not consumed one of another (Galatians 5:14-15).

Remember Jesus said whatever measure we use, we will mete (or get back). If we give a teaspoon of grace, we will receive only a teaspoon of grace (pressed down, shaken together, and running over). Matthew 18:21-35 tells the parable of a man who owed a huge debt. In today's figures, the debt this man owed would have been equivalent to 10 million dollars. When he is called on to pay it, he is forgiven of his debt. Later on, a different man owes the equivalent of a 20 dollar debt to the first man who, though he had been forgiven of a 10 million dollar debt, gave no forgiveness to the one who owed him 20 dollars. Instead, he sent him to the tormenters. Jesus said, *"likewise shall my heavenly Father do also unto you, if ye from your hearts forgive not every one his brother their trespasses"* (Matthew 18:35). How could a man who was forgiven $10,000,000.00 not forgive a man that owed him $20.00? When we think about the sin that Jesus has forgiven us of, our debt was bigger than the man who was forgiven of $10,000,000.00! It would take some kind of audacity to not forgive others!

Knowing that we will reap what we sow should motivate us to sow the right things. If we want to receive abundant grace, we need to make it our mission to give abundant grace. If we want to be dealt with in compassion, we must make it a priority to deal with others in compassion. Failure to deal with others in love means we have forgotten all of that we have been forgiven. Constructive criticism is a weighty thing. It is a great responsibility for believers that must not be handled lightly. We have a responsibility to God to make sure that we approach constructive criticism in wisdom.

Brethren, if a man be overtaken in a fault, ye which are spiritual, restore such an one in the spirit of meekness... (Galatians 6:1).

GOOD BEFORE BAD

A soft answer turneth away wrath: but grievous words stir up anger. The tongue of the wise useth knowledge aright: but the mouth of fools poureth out foolishness (Proverbs 15:1-2).

In the book of Revelation, Jesus wrote seven letters to seven churches. In the letter to one of those churches, He did not find anything bad to say about them. In another church, He did not find anything good. However in each case, He started with something positive before He reprimanded them. This idea is such a good tool for us to use in counseling or when we need to bring up an issue. Before we open our mouth to criticize, we need to find several things that person does well. No matter what we need to bring up, it can always be preceded by something positive.

If you cannot think of anything genuinely good to say before you attempt to offer constructive criticism, then you are not ready to offer any criticism. If you believe the Lord has prompted you to offer constructive criticism, ask yourself these questions:

- Have I prayed about this?
- Am I sure that the Lord is sending me?
- Is the timing right?

- Do I have Scripture to support what I am going to say?
- Am I respecting God's divine order?
- How will I start the conversation positively?
- Am I motivated by love?
- Is my goal to restoration or judgment?
- Have I evaluated my own life for the same issues? Am I walking uprightly with God?

THE GOAL OF CONSTRUCTIVE CRITICISM

Behold, for peace I had great bitterness: but thou hast in love to my soul delivered it from the pit of corruption: for thou hast cast all my sins behind thy back (Isaiah 38:17).

When we start to offer constructive criticism, we must make sure that it is Biblically based and motivated by love. In other words, it is counsel based on God's Spirit and Word. The goal of constructive criticism should always be restoration. A great way to make sure that the Spirit of God is motivating us is to assess our goals in the situation.

Think about what you want to say to the person and ask if it will help bring them restoration. There is nothing in the Word of God that qualifies us to cast judgment. We are called to bring restoration, and there is a right way to go about that. Being critical and judgmental is not the way. Jesus is the King of the universe. He is the Way, the Truth and the Life (John 14:6). He has all knowledge and wisdom, and He is the only one qualified to make judgments.

Consider this: when Jesus walked the earth, He had to know what it would take to get someone out of sin. In John 8:1-11, He encountered a woman who had been caught in adultery. According to the law, she was to be stoned. When she was cast at His feet He looked at her accusers and said, *"he who is without sin among you, let him cast the first stone."* This is amazing when you consider the implications. Jesus was the only one standing there who was qualified to make a judgment, because He was the only one standing there who did not have any sin in his life; yet He cast no stone. He did not condemn her. The Savior knew what to do and say to save that woman from her sin. He knew that mercy and compassion would set her on the path to restoration. He had the authority to condemn her, yet He forgave her saying, *"go and sin no more"* (v. 11). He knew that the grace she had received would draw her into a relationship with the Spirit of God, which would ultimately make her free from the sin she was in.

Proverbs 23:7 says that as a person thinks in his heart so is he. If we only tell people what sinners they are, it will get in their head that they are no good. When the temptation comes to continue in the sin, they will have nothing to resist it. They will only believe they are worthless. Jesus did not harp on the wrongs of the woman cast at His feet. He offered her mercy. Who are we not to do the same? We must point to the solution and not the problem. Keep in mind; it is the goodness of God that leads us to repentance (Romans 2:4). It makes the grace and mercy of God so much more beautiful when it is viewed in this light. God chooses to see the good in us because Jesus paid for the bad. He looked past our faults and saw our need.

Instead of harping on the flaws of one another, preach vision and speak life. Tell people who they are in Christ no matter where they are in the moment. This will give them something to aspire to. Why would anyone try for better if he or she did not believe they could rise to a better place? The reality is that because of Jesus' sacrifice, every single human being has hope, salvation and has the ability to get better. Build people up and they will want to be better. Keep this in mind next time you are tempted to be critical of your spouse, your children, or anyone in your life. Find something positive to say. When you do, you will find your house turn into a little sanctuary of God.

Keep the goals of your relationships clear. Do not allow yourself to become a critic. Criticism points out the sin and drives others away. Have restoration set before you always. Be mindful of your thoughts and intentional about love. Love works with others in the spirit of meekness. Love says, "I want this behind us." Someone who operates in love with patience and wisdom can be used by God to accomplish mighty things. Psalm 15 says that it is the person who is not critical that will abide in God's presence.

Lord, who shall abide in thy tabernacle? who shall dwell in thy holy hill? He that walketh uprightly, and worketh righteousness, and speaketh the truth in his heart. He that backbiteth not with his tongue, nor doeth evil to his neighbour, nor taketh up a reproach against his neighbor (Psalm 15:1-3).

And this I pray, that your love may abound yet more and more in knowledge and in all judgment (Philippians 1:9).

THE CRITICAL SPOUSE

But the fruit of the Spirit is love, joy, peace, longsuffering, gentleness, goodness, faith, Meekness, temperance: against such there is no law (Galatians 5:22-23).

Criticism will suck the joy right out of any relationship—certainly marriage. There are many things that can lead a spouse to becoming critical. An important thing to remember when you feel as though your spouse is being critical is that it is likely not about you. Criticism in marriage tends to manifest out of insecurity or the anxiety of not being in control. Critical people want power and this can be true in marriage.

There are many factors that can lead to criticism in marriage. I would like to share three of them with you. There are simple ways that we can rid our marriage of criticism and bring health to the relationship. However, it will require that we judge ourselves and try to understand our spouse's perspective.

Number 1, *irritation*. Is the criticism caused by irritation? Hunger, fatigue, illness or pain can lead to becoming critical. Have you ever heard someone say they were "*hangry*"? (That is to combine the word angry with hungry). I have to admit that I can become super-sensitive when I am hungry. Going without food or proper sleep can lead to becoming more critical of others. I am not condoning the attitude, but trying to explain it. When you recognize what might be the cause, you can respond without taking the criticism personally.

Number 2, *insight*. When we are mad, we lose insight. Instead of focusing inward on what the Lord would have us to do in a given situation, anger causes us to look outwardly. We become motivated to point out what we believe is causing our feelings and emotions. We begin to wonder who is to blame for the way we are feeling. It's part of our carnal nature to want to pass the blame, rather than accepting responsibility. Sadly, if this is not dealt with, criticism towards others (particularly your spouse) is increased. The best way to deal with angry feelings is to gain some insight. Pray and ask the Lord for wisdom. Look inwardly. Take time to search your heart, calm your mind and settle your emotions before addressing your spouse.

Number 3, *ignorance*. When we refuse to understand our spouse's position or perspective, we give life to the spirit of criticism. We should always be willing to put ourselves in our spouse's position and offer the benefit of the doubt. If you feel like your spouse does not see your position, learn to respond in a way that will calm the situation without raising the intensity.

There is a way to acknowledge a person's criticism without agreeing with it. It is important to let your spouse know that they have been heard and that you understand their feelings. Many times, simply allowing them to speak their mind without interruption will do much to help the situation. This does not mean that you must agree. It means that you are showing them the respect and honor of listening. The right response can create a buffer until sound reasoning is accomplished and the issue is resolved. I have witnessed my wife, Chrissy, use such buffering until I got my bearings. In many cases the issue was not even worth repeating but ended with an apology and request for forgiveness—all because of the way she responded to my criticism. In many cases couples argue more about the reaction than the original complaint. It's important to pause. Let your spouse know they were heard, but don't react.

One way to refrain from a critical spirit is the use of the words "I feel" rather than "you". When addressing your complaint with "you," your spouse will, by nature, take on the mode of defense. However, when sharing your heart, by saying, "I feel", you open the door for your spouse to understand your heart without feeling like they've been accused or condemned.

I have heard it said that when one feels attacked they respond with either, *"flight, freeze or fight."* *Flight,* they run from the situation; *Freeze,* they lock up emotionally and have nothing to say; *Fight,* they respond in retaliation. None of these are healthy responses.

Effective communication is done in love and brings forth joy. I believe that is why joy is listed behind love as a fruit of the Spirit (Galatians 5:22). However, the voice of criticism will strip joy from any relationship—especially marriage. It is vital to a healthy marriage that couples engage in healthy communication without criticism.

There is no such thing as a perfect spouse. We must be willing to offer grace and walk in love. It is how we relate in the midst of a critical spirit that truly conveys our love. *"He that covereth a transgression seeketh love; but he that repeateth a matter separateth very friends"* (Proverbs 17:9). Sadly, there are many marriages that are hurting because of an unwillingness to stop repeating a matter. Consider the verses below. They make it very clear that continuous harping on something leads to separation whereas love covers.

> *Hatred stirreth up strifes: but love covereth all sins* (Proverbs 10:12).

> *And above all things have fervent charity among yourselves: for charity [love] shall cover the multitude of sins* (1 Peter 4:8).

A MULTITUDE OF COUNSELORS

> *Where no counsel is, the people fall: but in the multitude of counselors there is safety* (Proverbs 11:14).

In the book of Isaiah, God lists seven different anointings that come on us when we are walking in-tune with the Holy Spirit. These are attributes of the Holy Spirit. These things should exist in us if we are in the presence of God and walking in His anointing. Any one of His anointings will remove burdens and destroy yokes. One of these attributes is the anointing of counsel.

> *And the **spirit of the Lord** shall rest upon him, the spirit of **wisdom** and **understanding**, the spirit of **counsel** and **might**, the spirit of **knowledge** and of the **fear of the Lord*** (Isaiah 11:2, emphasis added).

Counsel is specific advice or information that helps one to determine a course of action. As Christians, we are all able to give Biblical counsel to some degree in that we can point others to what the Bible says. If we know Jesus and if we are spending time in His Word, we will walk in His anointing.

> *And it shall come to pass in that day, that his burden shall be taken away from off thy shoulder, and his yoke from off thy neck, and the yoke shall be destroyed because of the anointing* (Isaiah 10:27).

This verse defines the anointing of God as the burden-removing, yoke-destroying power of God. The anointing is something we as Christians should be familiar with because we have been called to operate under the power of God's Spirit. When the Holy Spirit rubs off on us a characteristic of Himself, that is called the anointing. We are to take on the anointing of the Holy Spirit.

"Iron sharpeneth iron..." (Proverbs 27:17).

Believers need to be around other believers. The health, success, or failure of your life will be largely based on your inner circle—those that are most influential in your life. We need to invest in relationships with people who will encourage our faith and believe along with us.

Jesus had an inner circle. Though He had 12 disciples, Peter, James and John were with Him all the time. When He was about to raise a woman from the dead, or go up to the Mount of Transfiguration, all 12 probably would not have believed with Him; but Peter, James and John did. God uses your inner circle that He has placed in your life to help direct you and lead you.

> *Blessed is the man that walketh not in the counsel of the ungodly, nor standeth in the way of sinners, nor sitteth in the seat of the scornful* (Psalms 1:1).

> *The way of a fool is right in his own eyes: but he that hearkeneth unto counsel is wise* (Proverbs 12:15).

Many times we have the answer down deep inside and we only need the right counsel to draw it out.

> *Counsel in the heart of man is like deep water; but a man of understanding will draw it out* (Proverbs 20:5).

Godly counsel will always be based on the Word of God. It will turn you from the wrong way to the right way. There are no lone-rangers in ministry. God will put a safety net of people around you that He can anoint.

Do not neglect God's Word. His Word is His counsel. God may have 100 ways He can get the right information to you at any given moment. Keep in mind that, though He may use them, He does not need all those ways. The sure way is always the Word.

> *But if they had stood in my counsel, and had caused my people to hear my words, then they should have turned them from their evil way, and from the evil of their doings* (Jeremiah 23:22).

> *Then the people of the land weakened the hands of the people of Judah, and troubled them in building, And hired counselors against them, to frustrate their purpose* (Ezra 4:4-5).

Be careful who you accept counsel from. Criticism is strategic in the enemy's plan. Just as they hired "counselors" in the book of Ezra to criticize the people of Judah, the enemy will plant critics in your life who criticize everything you do to frustrate or hinder your purpose. It is okay to look at the fruit of someone's life before you accept their counsel. Jesus said that you would know a tree by its fruit. If someone is not living a Godly life and producing fruit, it is probably not wise to take counsel from them. You can treat them with love, but you do not have to accept their counsel.

> *Beware of false prophets, which come to you in sheep's clothing, but inwardly they are ravening wolves. Ye shall know them by their fruits. Do men gather grapes of thorns, or figs of thistles? Even so every good tree bringeth forth good fruit; but a corrupt tree bringeth forth evil fruit. A good tree cannot*

bring forth evil fruit, neither can a corrupt tree bring forth good fruit. Every tree that bringeth not forth good fruit is hewn down, and cast into the fire. Wherefore by their fruits ye shall know them (Matthew 7:15-20).

Don't let yourself get caught up in people bondage. You cannot please everyone. People may not realize what kind of damage they are doing when they offer criticism under the guise of 'counsel'. They may not have taken the time to pray and seek God. Many people say what they are thinking. They do not take the time to see if what they are going to say is edifying. Some people will criticize as a means to control. We are not obligated to accept all advice that comes to us. We are obligated to weigh it against the Word of God. If you are on the receiving end of ungodly counsel or criticism, do not allow yourself to worry over it. Once you stop yourself from worrying about it, that critical person loses their control over you. If you allow negative criticism to reside in your mind, it will have the opposite effect of anointed counsel. Do not let the enemy control you through negative criticism.

In the midst of the social media frenzy, it can be hard to avoid other's criticism. You might need to 'unfriend' or stop following some people on social media forums. Do not give the enemy that platform. Think about it like this, if we would spend more time with our face in His Book, we would not be moved by what is on Facebook. Do not give those with impure motives a voice into your life.

Hide me from the secret counsel of the wicked; from the insurrection of the workers of iniquity: Who whet their tongue like a sword, and bend their bows to shoot their arrows, even

bitter words: That they may shoot in secret at the perfect:
suddenly do they shoot at him, and fear not (Psalms 64:2-4).

The enemy plants secret counselors in our lives whose only objective
is to criticize and destroy. Mindfully, we cannot allow the enemy to use
us to criticize and destroy others. Consider the fact that if it were given
the authority to point out others faults, no one would be able to stand.

If thou, Lord, shouldest mark iniquities, O Lord, who shall
stand? (Psalms 130:3).

Discern between those who God has anointed to bring counsel in
your life and those the enemy has brought to discourage you. The counsel
that God uses to shape and direct your life will come out of a pure motive.
Do not let your critics plague you. In Isaiah 9, Jesus is called Counselor.

For unto us a child is born, unto us a son is given: and the
government shall be upon his shoulder: and his name shall
be called Wonderful, **Counselor***, The mighty God, The ever-*
lasting Father, The Prince of Peace (v. 6, emphasis added).

The Holy Spirit is our ultimate Counselor. The Bible says that we
have an unction in us, or an anointing, to understand God's wisdom and
know what to do with it. In most cases, your critics come from outside
your circle; your counselors come from within your circle. A true friend
or counselor would certainly never use a public forum to 'help' you. The
Holy Spirit will help you discern the difference between friend and foe.

But ye have an unction from the Holy One, and ye know all things. I have not written unto you because ye know not the truth, but because ye know it, and that no lie is of the truth (1 John 2:20-21).

If you are a born again believer, you have the truth inside you because you have the Holy Spirit inside you. The Word and prayer will be the keys to draw it out. Any anointed counsel will testify, confirm and agree with the Word of God and the knowledge of Him.

Have not I written to thee excellent things in counsels and knowledge, That I might make thee know the certainty of the words of truth; that thou mightest answer the words of truth to them that send unto thee? (Proverbs 22:22-21).

Hear; for I will speak of excellent things; and the opening of my lips shall be right things (Proverbs 8:6).

And this I pray, that your love may abound yet more and more in knowledge and in all judgment; That ye may approve things that are excellent; that ye may be sincere and without offence till the day of Christ (Philippians 1:9-10).

The critic wants to expose sin. The counselor wants to cover it, and to see God correct it through His love, word and wisdom. *"Hatred stirreth up strifes: but love covereth all sins"* (Proverbs 10:12). The critic is the accuser— Jesus is the restorer. When it comes to our judgments and counsel, we want to be motivated by love.

For he shall have judgment without mercy, that hath shewed no mercy; and mercy rejoiceth against judgment (James 2:13).

That literally means that mercy has victory over judgment. In the battle between mercy and judgment, mercy wins every time! It means we are to let mercy take precedence over judgment, no matter how justified we feel. We must be sensitive to mercy before we give counsel. Mercy is larger, and it always trumps judgment. Psalms 85:10 is a great description of what happened on the cross. Jesus was able to give mercy because He took our judgment. We cannot be critics who point our finger and condemn. We are to be counselors who believe in others, who pray for them and encourage them to come out of whatever they are in. Just as God has done for us, we need to choose to see others beyond their condition. This will enable us to lead people in love to restoration.

Mercy and truth are met together; righteousness and peace have kissed each other (Psalm 85:10).

Chapter 11

LOVE UNFAILING, TRUTH UNCOMPROMISED

---◆---

Jesus taught that His disciples would be known for their love. John 13:35 says, *"By this shall all men know that ye are my disciples, if ye have love one to another."* I can only imagine what a difference could be made by those who name the Name of Jesus if we all walked in the love of God. Jesus gave us specific instruction on what type of love we were to walk in. In the previous verse, He states, *"A new commandment I give unto you, That ye love one another; as I have loved you, that ye also love one another"* (John 13:34). The love we are called to show others is the same love that He has given to us!

We will never know nor understand the power of God's love if we do not choose to abide in Him. My wife once said, "When we try to do this Christian life without abiding in Him, we will only become religious." The love of God is the fruit of His Spirit (Galatians 5:22). As a matter of fact, it is the first-fruit of the Spirit. If the first-fruit be holy, the lump is holy (Romans 11:16). We will never see the fruit of joy, peace, longsuffering, gentleness, goodness, faith, meekness and temperance if we are not abiding in Him and walking in love.

If ye abide in me, and my words abide in you, ye shall ask what ye will, and it shall be done unto you. Herein is my Father glorified, that ye bear much fruit; so shall ye be my disciples. As the Father hath loved me, so have I loved you: continue ye in my love (John 15:7-9).

I truly believe that a critical spirit has worked against our witness, preventing the love of God from manifesting in our lives, relationships, churches and ministries. Jesus was no stranger to criticism. He was constantly criticized for His acts and teachings. It is interesting to study the source of His criticism. Self-righteous and religious men constantly criticized Jesus. The Pharisees and Sadducees were constantly following Jesus around and knit-picking His every word and deed. These men believed themselves to be higher and greater than the "common" man. They wore their religious garments and made long prayers to be seen of men. Sadly, there are many who fit their description today.

The self-righteously religious person is more concerned about the appearance of something rather than its true condition. This fallen world is so broken that it believes a man can be judged by the color of his skin. I am reminded of the words of Dr. Martin Luther King, "I look to a day when people will not be judged by the color of their skin, but by the content of their character." The color of one's skin neither makes them right nor wrong—It is our character that defines who we are. Sadly, there are many who can't make righteous judgments because of bias and prejudice. We live in a world that chooses to judge based on appearance rather than condition or character.

We see prejudice in literally every walk of life. It goes far beyond ethnicity. Men and women are judged and criticized for a plethora of reasons.

Jesus corrected such bias. He taught us not to judge the outward appearance of man because it does not reflect the condition of his heart.

> *Woe unto you, scribes and Pharisees, hypocrites! for ye make clean the outside of the cup and of the platter, but within they are full of extortion and excess. Thou blind Pharisee, cleanse first that which is within the cup and platter, that the outside of them may be clean also* (Matthew 23:37-40).

Simply put, the way someone looks on the outside does not necessarily reflect the condition of his or her soul. We must not allow the Pharisee's mindset to creep into our lives. This religious crowd constantly criticized Jesus and His response was that they were "hypocrites!" We are not called to sit in the seat of self-righteous judgment.

Jesus received much of His criticism because of His love and association with "sinners." His miracles were centered around the broken, poor, sick and oppressed. In today's culture, it might be hard for us to understand the impact of Jesus' healing miracles in that day. It was a different time. They believed that sickness, infirmity and disease came as punishment upon a person for their sins. A sick person might be viewed as one that is paying for their wrong deeds. Sadly, for many, it merited the suffering of man. This is why there is not one case in Scripture were Jesus was not able to heal. His healing was a demonstration of something much bigger—forgiveness!

This is evident when the disciples asked Jesus about a man that was born blind. *"And his disciples asked him, saying, Master, who did sin, this man, or his parents, that he was born blind?"* (John 9:1). They started to consider why the man was born blind, if blindness (being a type of infirmity) came as a result of sin. They concluded that it must have been his parents fault. Jesus responded that his blindness had nothing to do with his or his parents' sin. *"Jesus answered, Neither hath this man sinned, nor his parents: but that the works of God should be made manifest in him"* (v. 3).

You can see why the religious crowd did not honor Jesus' healing of the sick, maimed, blind, or oppressed. In their self-righteous minds, the brokenness of these individuals' was something they deserved. They mistakenly believed that the sick had brought their sicknesses upon themselves. As I read the story of the blind man being healed, it is obvious to me that they did not want to believe that he was "born blind." It makes sense that they would have a hard time with it. To accept that he was born blind would negate their belief that he deserved his condition. Sadly, that same mindset exists today. There are many who still believe that sickness is a punishment for sin. I love the response of the blind man at the end of the story. *"He answered and said, Whether he be a sinner or no, I know not: one thing I know, that, whereas I was blind, now I see"* (John 9:25).

This opens up another thought. How many people today will criticize the methods of ministries and churches, yet they overlook the result or the fruit that ministry or church is producing? They do not care that souls are being saved. They act exactly like the religious crowd of Jesus' day. Instead of acknowledging the miraculous healing power of Jesus—they criticized. They tried to entrap Him, calling Him a sinner (because He had worked this miracle on the Sabbath day, v. 16). This is typical of the critical and self-righteous. They did not care that the blind had received his sight. They were too concerned with finding fault.

As a pastor, I hear every criticism you can imagine—everything from doctrinal arguments to style of worship to clothing (including not wearing a tie). I have heard criticism on the lighting in the sanctuary, the color of the carpet, the age of leaders—you name it; I have heard the criticism! What is so sad is how the critics overlook the results. The number of lives we see come to Christ is amazing! The critic will overlook the results of lives saved, baptized, and liberated by the power of the Gospel and the knowledge of His Word. Instead, they are content to sit back and criticize the methods.

The story of Jesus healing the blind man and the criticism offered by the religious crowd is a perfect example of the danger of being overly critical and judgmental. Where is love in that story? Where is the compassion? Where is the desire for broken man to find his wholeness in Jesus? If we are to see revival and witness the power of the Gospel, we must break the mindset of self-righteous criticism and love unconditionally!

> *And it came to pass, as Jesus sat at meat in the house, behold, many publicans and sinners came and sat down with him and his disciples. And when the Pharisees saw it, they said unto his disciples, Why eateth your Master with publicans and sinners? But when Jesus heard that, he said unto them, They that be whole need not a physician, but they that are sick. But go ye and learn what that meaneth, I will have mercy, and not sacrifice: for I am not come to call the righteous, but sinners to repentance* (Matthew 9:11).

In this verse, Jesus was criticized for eating with sinners. In reality, He was a guest along with all who were present. He was eating at Matthew's house. He had called Matthew, a tax collector, into His ministry. I can see Matthew inviting all of his friends over to celebrate his new walk. Jesus takes opportunity to reach out to those present. True to their usual behavior, the Pharisees found fault with this. "*Why eateth your Master with publicans and sinners?*" they said. I love Jesus' response, "*I am not come to call the righteous, but sinners to repentance*" (v. 11). Jesus' mission was and is to save the lost. *"For the Son of man is come to seek and to save that which was lost"* (Luke 19:10). We are called to share in this mission—that's why it is called the "Great Commission" (Matthew 28:19-20). We are co-partners in Jesus' mission to save the lost.

SPEAKING THE TRUTH IN LOVE

But speaking the truth in love, may grow up into him in all things, which is the head, even Christ (Ephesians 4:15).

Clearly, we are called to speak the truth in love. I believe that our love should always be the motivation behind our counsel and ministering. I was sharing this with a dear friend and member recently when he reminded me of how Jesus' instruction came because of His love.

In Mark 10, we read where Jesus gave a rich man direction. The counsel may have not been what he wanted to hear, but it was offered in love. This man came to Jesus desiring knowledge. Jesus, motivated by love, told him the truth.

*Then Jesus beholding him **loved him**, and said unto him, One thing thou lackest: go thy way, sell whatsoever thou hast, and give to the poor, and thou shalt have treasure in heaven: and come, take up the cross, and follow me* (Mark 10:21, emphasis added).

How many people truly offer counsel based on truth and love? I believe it is vital that we search our hearts for the love of God. I believe that until we are motivated by love, our 'truth' will not penetrate the hearts of men. People will receive more of what you 'know', when they 'know' you genuinely care. The difference between effective counsel and ministry is made by the motive of the counselor or minister. Preachers can duplicate another's message, but that is not to say they can echo the heart behind it. I am convinced that without love, we are no more than sounding brass, or tinkling cymbals (1 Corinthians 13:1).

Some may view this "judge not" mindset as an "anything goes" ideology. That is simply not the truth. I have personally observed the power of truth when spoken in love. One does not have to compromise truth when acting or speaking in love. Acting in love will never compromise truth. These two are met together by the Spirit of God.

Our society is filled with acceptance of things that God's Word clearly defines as unacceptable. We can approach these issues with the truth of the Word of God in a hateful and condemning nature, or we can share these truths motivated by a love for those who have fallen into deception. The truth will liberate the most calloused and sinful heart when the motive behind our words is love—love for the souls of mankind. Sadly, I am concerned that many in the church-world are using the truth in a condemning fashion with no love for the lost souls that Jesus gave His life for! I have heard many testimonies of lives who changed after attending Word of God Ministries. I will not compromise the truth of His Word. Some might think that those living a compromised lifestyle might find the Word offensive and leave. Yet I have found that souls are responding, repenting and accepting Jesus as Savior. People are being liberated by the power of His love! There is no doubt that we can minister the truth and, at the same time, be motivated by love.

SAVED BY GRACE

For by grace are ye saved through faith; and that not of your-
selves: it is the gift of God: Not of works, lest any man should
boast (Ephesians 2:8-9).

We cannot forget that our salvation is by God's grace. If we could have saved ourselves, Jesus could have stayed in heaven! I have met those who preached "grace" but were actually critical "law givers." I truly believe that one can view the Law through the lens of grace without being caught up in legalism. The Law was necessary. It led us to grace. Without the Law there would be no knowledge of sin (Romans 3:20). Without the knowledge of sin, we would not see the need for salvation offered through Jesus Christ. *"Moreover the law entered, that the offence might abound. But where sin abounded, grace did much more abound"* (Romans 5:20). I encourage all believers to study Romans Chapter 5. This chapter clarifies the work of redemption. It takes you from the fall of man (the original sin of Adam) to the righteousness of Jesus Christ. By one man's sin (Adam), we all became sinners. By the righteousness of One (Jesus), we all have the chance to be made righteous (Romans 5:12-18).

It should be hard for an individual who knows that they have been saved by grace to place others in a box of legalism. Abstaining from a legalistic mindset does not mean that Christians do not live by the standards of God's commandments—we merely recognize that our compliance to His commandments does not merit salvation. Romans 3 makes this abundantly clear. Notice the following passage:

Now we know that what things soever the law saith, it saith
to them who are under the law: that every mouth may be

stopped, and all the world may become guilty before God. Therefore by the deeds of the law there shall no flesh be justified in his sight: for by the law is the knowledge of sin. But now the righteousness of God without the law is manifested, being witnessed by the law and the prophets; Even the righteousness of God which is by faith of Jesus Christ unto all and upon all them that believe: for there is no difference: For all have sinned, and come short of the glory of God; Being justified freely by his grace through the redemption that is in Christ Jesus: Whom God hath set forth to be a propitiation through faith in his blood, to declare his righteousness for the remission of sins that are past, through the forbearance of God; To declare, I say, at this time his righteousness: that he might be just, and the justifier of him which believeth in Jesus. Where is boasting then? It is excluded. By what law? of works? Nay: but by the law of faith. Therefore we conclude that a man is justified by faith without the deeds of the law (Romans 3:19-28).

Verse 31 goes on to say that we do not make the law void through faith—but rather we establish it. Jesus taught true righteousness would exceed the performance of the law. For example, the Law forbids murder. Yet Jesus taught, do not hate, and equated hate with murder (Matthew 5:21-22). My point is that though we seek to honor God and His Word, we can never forget that no matter how we may labor to honor it, we fall short—we are sinners. It was only by His grace that we could be saved. We must not take a legalistic position and criticize others with a judgment that has not been given to us. We all needed the same grace to know salvation. As Christians, let us be ministers of grace without compromising the standards and convictions of righteousness. That may seem difficult; but again, Jesus showed us the way. As we read earlier in John 8:4-11, a woman caught in adultery was brought to Jesus. The law was voiced; her accusers condemned her. Jesus, without condoning her actions, said, *"He that is without sin among you, let him first cast a stone at her"* (v. 7). Her accusers walked away because they all had sin. Jesus told the woman, *"Neither do I condemn thee: go, and sin no more"* (v. 11). The law condemned her but grace saved her! Jesus was the only one present without sin and He condemned not. Oh, what grace! Who are we to judge and condemn others? Are any of us without sin? Jesus showed us a better way—grace! I believe the power of grace enables us to live a life of righteousness.

TWO'S COMPANY, THREE'S A CROWD

*Again I say unto you, That if **two of you shall agree** on earth as touching any thing that they shall ask, it shall be done for them of my Father which is in heaven. For where two or **three are gathered** together in my name, there am I in the midst of them* (Matthew 18:19-20, emphasis added).

Early on in my walk of faith, I was strongly urged to isolate myself from anyone who did not believe exactly as I was taught. I heard condemning messages about other churches and ministers that did not carry the same denominational tag. In my heart, I knew some things I was hearing did not line up with the heart of Christ. Sadly, many believers have allowed the enemy to keep them divided and harping on what they do not agree on. We should be walking in unity. Its better to focus on the things that we do agree on. I was once asked to write an article on the answer to racism. I had a news outlet ask me to share my convictions on racism (which I believe to be unacceptable), and to share on how I was able to pastor an integrated church. In that article, I addressed the "Common Denominator"—Jesus! It is better to focus on what *unites* than on what divides.

I have strong fundamental convictions when it comes to God's Word. I do not intend to compromise my convictions. I believe in the virgin birth. I believe Jesus died to pay the debt of our sin. I believe Jesus lived a sinless life. I believe He was raised from the dead! I believe that He is returning again! I believe He sent His Spirit to us on the Day of Pentecost. I believe the Bible is the inerrant Word of God. I believe that Jesus is the Manifested Word of God. I believe that salvation is in NO OTHER NAME but the NAME OF JESUS! I believe that we should live by His Word. I believe in forgiveness, baptism, and the Great Commission to reach the world for Christ. I could continue with this list. In my heart, these are fundamental doctrines of the faith—fundamental beliefs that I would never waiver on.

I have met plenty of people who agreed with fundamental doctrines like those that I have listed above, yet differed on other interpretations or positions. For example, I have met those who differed on their ideas about women, worship, tithes, etc. (only to name a few).

Have you ever heard the statement, "Two's company, three's a crowd"? I believe there can be some truth to that. As parents of four, Chrissy and I have seen the reality of that with our children. Two of them can be playing well until a third steps in the activity. In the verse quoted above, Jesus used the words *"two of you shall agree"* and *"three are gathered."* It is easy for two to agree. But once you start adding to that number, the harder it is to agree. You may still "gather", but agreement becomes harder. Can we be mature enough to agree to disagree without condemning the other view? Can we speak the truth in love and walk away, letting the Holy Spirit do the rest? I made my mind up long ago that I am not going to use my energy trying to debate over a topic that another wants to argue. I make my position in His Word clear and leave it at that. I am not going to point my finger, condemn, or get in the flesh over it. God has not called us to judge the law—we are to be doers of the Word. *"Speak not evil one of another, brethren. He that speaketh evil of his brother, and judgeth his brother, speaketh evil of the law, and judgeth the law:* **but if thou judge the law, thou art not a doer of the law, but a judge"** (James 4:11, emphasis added).

I have never understood those who will invest hours attacking someone for a different view. In my opinion, it would be better to use that energy to win the lost to Christ. What are we accomplishing when we bite and devour one another? (See Galatians 5:14-15). If one chooses to honor God's Word in tithing, is it really someone else's concern or right to criticize simply because they do not believe in tithing? I use this as an example for a reason. I have been in ministry for more than half of my life. There are a handful of topics that I have seen believers get divided and plum fleshy over. In their arguments and debates, they send the wrong message both to the lost and to the young in the faith. It sets the wrong example. Again, I wish this same energy were used to minister to the lost! I remember one week where I was ridiculed for teaching on a certain topic. At the end of the message over 30 souls accepted Christ. Do you think the critic mentioned those saved? Not hardly. The critic was too busy debating the message. Does that remind you of anything? (The Pharisee's criticism of Jesus when He had healed the blind.)

Let's face it. Some people do not want to live by God's Word. They want to come to church so they can feel good about themselves. Oftentimes, when the Word strikes an area that needs addressing, people will turn and attack the pastor. Jesus said, *"Whosoever therefore shall break one of these least commandments, and shall teach men so, he shall be called the least in the kingdom of heaven: but whosoever shall do and teach them, the same shall be called great in the kingdom of heaven"* (Matthew 5:19). There are those who will spend countless hours trying to convince people not to honor certain aspects of the Word of God as they argue their own ideology. Sadly, they will even turn and condemn anyone who does not believe as they do. According to Jesus, the least in the Kingdom are those who break the least of His commandments and teach others to do so. The greatest in the Kingdom are those who do obey His commandments and teach others to do so. We must make up our minds on where we want to be in His Kingdom. If you are going to live and teach His word, prepare for criticism.

There will always be those who gather in our congregation and yet not agree with the teachings, ministry, and so forth. As a pastor, I must rely on the Holy Spirit to convince (John 16:8-13). My responsibility is to speak the truth in love. I have been challenged by this. I have had individuals approach me who wanted to be sure I saw their life-style choices or knew their opposing position to my teachings. I have sensed they are expecting me to take it personally, judge, or condemn. However, I have chosen to walk in love (without compromising the truth). What have I discovered by doing this? For starters, the critics leave you alone once they discover they cannot control you. As far as the lost sinner who dares to be flagrant, I have seen these same lives changed by the power of the Gospel! I have never met anyone that God could not save, because I have never met anyone that He did not love! We must refuse to let people move us away from love. Some of the easiest people to reach are those who know their sin. The self-righteous who will not acknowledge their own faults are the ones who reject the power of the Gospel.

You will find that Jesus reserved His sharp reprimands for the religious and self-righteous, while He offered grace and salvation to those who were broken. Pointing our fingers and condemning the lost will not bring them to salvation—it will simply drive them away. We can stand for the Word, hold to our convictions, preach the truth and love people at the same time. It is the only way—it is Jesus' way!

BUILDING WALLS OR BUILDING BRIDGES

Wherefore henceforth know we no man after the flesh: yea, though we have known Christ after the flesh, yet now henceforth know we him no more. Therefore if any man be in Christ, he is a new creature: old things are passed away; behold, all things are become new. And all things are of God, who hath reconciled us to himself by Jesus Christ, and hath given to us the ministry of reconciliation; To wit, that God was in Christ, reconciling the world unto himself, not imputing their trespasses unto them; and hath committed unto us the word of reconciliation. Now then we are ambassadors for Christ, as though God did beseech you by us: we pray you in Christ's stead, be ye reconciled to God. For he hath made him to be sin for us, who knew no sin; that we might be made the righteousness of God in him (2 Corinthians 5:16-21).

As believers and ambassadors for Christ, do we want to build walls or bridges? Are we called to drive away the lost or bridge the gap through the Gospel of Jesus Christ? Let us make up our minds to be bridge-builders! Jesus is the mediator between God and man. Our responsibility is to represent Him and bring the lost to His saving grace. This can be done through speaking the truth in love. We have been given the *"ministry of reconciliation"* (v. 18). Criticism builds walls while love and truth builds bridges. Criticism isolates. Love unites.

From the earliest days of the church, we see the struggle of overcoming the walls of division and bridging the gap between God and man, and man with humanity. This world is divisive in nature. Look around; turn on the news. This world is divided! In the midst of a divided world, we have been given the *"word of reconciliation"* (v. 19). The Word of God is a living tool, an active sword, divinely crafted to accomplish God's desire of unity and reconciliation. We can be confident when we use it, because its power is not dependent on us or on how skilled we are at wielding it. The power in the Word of God is made mighty by the Spirit of God who lives in us. Let your faith be in Him.

God has not called us to isolate ourselves within our walls while pointing our fingers out of our small windows and condemning those who are not like us. He has called us to be bridge builders and bridge the gap between fallen man and a merciful Savior. We have been given the ministry of reconciliation.

In the Book of Acts, we see where the early church faced the struggle of reconciliation. When God spoke to Peter about ministering to the Gentiles, he was hesitant. As a Jew, he had adopted the mindset of separation. Living sanctified is not the equivalent of living superior. We are not superior to others simply because we have been saved. It is because we have been saved by grace that we are even able to stand! It would appear that Peter thought more of himself than he should have. Thinking too highly of ourselves leads us to thinking too little of others. God told Peter to call no man "common." This means do not look down on anyone, or think that you are superior to anyone.

> *And he said unto them, Ye know how that it is an unlawful*
> *thing for a man that is a Jew to keep company, or come*

*unto one of another nation; but God hath shewed me that
I should not call any man common or unclean* (Acts 10:28).

He went on to say, *"Of a truth I perceive that God is no respecter of persons"* (v. 34). This moment, where Peter (a Jew) extends the Gospel to a Gentile family, is a landmark moment for the church. Here, not only do we see the Gospel bridging the gap between God and the Gentiles, but we also see the Gospel bridging the gap between the Jews and the Gentiles. Prior to this era, there was only separation.

Peter, a Jew, saw the Gentiles as "common." God had to rid that mindset from Peter. Is there a race or group of people that you view as "common" or less than your own group, calling or ethnicity? We cannot bridge this gap until we lose that ideology.

In this region, particularly, I believe there are two avenues in which the enemy has wrought division—race and (bad) religion. We as a society have allowed the strongest of criticisms to be planted in our hearts by one or the other. There are countless lives who cannot see the good in one another because of racism. Our communities are plagued with racist and prejudice mindsets. Once the stronghold of racism is established in the mind, it only seeks to strengthen itself. The prejudiced mind looks for bricks that will strengthen the stronghold of his or her worldview. Any report that strengthens the ideology of racism will add a brick to the stronghold. If the report does not strengthen the stronghold, it is rejected. That is the power of the strongholds of criticism. It is constantly looking to be validated and strengthened.

The second means of division is based on man-made religion. The Samaritan woman that met Jesus in John 4 is a perfect example. She wanted to know why He would speak to her because He was a Jew. She challenged him on which mount in Israel should be the place of worship.

There is some history here that I will not get into; but to sum it up, the Jews and the Samaritans were divided on which place was acceptable in temple worship. Does that sound odd? Well it should not. How many people have been ostracized for where they attend church? Just recently, a woman who attended another church confronted me in public. She said, "You're stealing our members." I spoke to her briefly and kindly (trying to defuse her tone) and then moved on. How can we lead the lost to Christ and the church when they witness our arguments and debates about where we should and should not be attending? Instead of debating where we should attend, we should be inviting the lost to attend with us. Some members have told me that their own family has alienated them because they attend Word of God Ministries. Does any of this sound like Christ? Certainly not! Then it should not exist within Christianity. Let us not allow our places of worship to be the subject of criticism.

This world is crying out for something real—something relevant. In a world of relativity, people long for truth. In a world of vanity, people are searching for substance. It is time for the Body of Christ to rise up in the power of His Spirit and the purity of His love!

> *Jesus said unto him, Thou shalt love the Lord thy God with all thy heart, and with all thy soul, and with all thy mind. This is the first and great commandment. And the second is like unto it, Thou shalt love thy neighbour as thyself. On these two commandments hang all the law and the prophets* (Matthew 22:37-40).

Do you want to honor God? Do you want His purpose done in your life? Do you want to see a manifestation of all law and prophecy fulfilled?

Jesus tells us how to do it. Love God with everything in you and love your neighbor as yourself!

WHO IS MY NEIGHBOR?

The following passage is a little lengthy, but I want you to see what Jesus said about loving your neighbor.

> *And, behold, a certain lawyer stood up, and tempted him, saying, Master, what shall I do to inherit eternal life? He said unto him, What is written in the law? how readest thou? And he answering said, Thou shalt love the Lord thy God with all thy heart, and with all thy soul, and with all thy strength, and with all thy mind; and thy neighbour as thyself. And he said unto him, Thou hast answered right: this do, and thou shalt live. But he, willing to justify himself, said unto Jesus, And who is my neighbour? And Jesus answering said, A certain man went down from Jerusalem to Jericho, and fell among thieves, which stripped him of his raiment, and wounded him, and departed, leaving him half dead. And by chance there came down a certain priest that way: and when he saw him, he passed by on the other side. And likewise a Levite, when he was at the place, came and looked on him, and passed by on the other side. But a certain Samaritan, as he journeyed, came where he was: and when he saw him, he had compassion on him, And went to him, and bound up his wounds, pouring in oil and wine, and set him on his own beast, and brought him to an inn, and took care of him. And on the morrow when he*

departed, he took out two pence, and gave them to the host, and said unto him, Take care of him; and whatsoever thou spendest more, when I come again, I will repay thee. Which now of these three, thinkest thou, was neighbour unto him that fell among the thieves? And he said, He that shewed mercy on him. Then said Jesus unto him, Go, and do thou likewise (Luke 10:25-37).

Notice the man's response when Jesus told him to love his neighbor—*"who is my neighbor?"* This man said this to justify himself. He wanted to choose his neighbor. Jesus taught that his neighbor was any man in need! In this story, this Jew was told the good neighbor was a Samaritan! This illustrates that our neighbors may not look like us, live where we live, or do what we do. But when we have opportunity to minister the Gospel, we have come across a neighbor that we are to love as ourselves.

In this story, the Good Samaritan represents Jesus. The man beaten and robbed represents fallen man. The inn represents the church. The innkeeper represents our pastors and ministers. It is time we go out and bring fallen man to a place of love, care and restoration! Jesus said, *"Go, and do thou likewise"* (v. 37).

FREELY RECEIVED—FREELY GIVE

Enough with harsh and demeaning words of criticism! Enough with the self-righteous hypocrisies! Enough with the condemning judgments! There is a lost world out there that needs the knowledge of a Savior who loves them. He laid down His life that we might be saved! May the church rise, may the church love, may the church speak the truth and trust the Spirit to draw and convict!

We must lay down our agendas. We must let go of our pride. God resists the proud and He gives grace to the humble (James 4:6). We do not have to know it all. We do not have anything to prove. Let us lay down our selfish causes at the foot of a blood-stained cross and take up a new life of sacrificial love! Let us quit expecting more from others than we could ever provide ourselves. Let us be quick to repent and quick to forgive! Let our song be, *"Amazing grace! How sweet the sound that saved a wretch like me! I once was lost, but now am found; Was blind, but now I see"* [*Amazing Grace*, John Newton].

Let us go into the highways and bring in *"the poor, and the maimed, and the halt, and the blind"*—that His house might be filled! (See Luke 14:21). Let us love the unlovable, embrace the broken, lift up the fallen, feed the hungry, clothe the naked and welcome the cast-out! Our sin never intimidated God; let us not be intimidated by those caught in sin! Let us advance the Kingdom, preach the Gospel, lift up the blood-stained banner of the cross and win souls for Jesus, the Savior of the world!

Our own righteousness is as filthy rags (Isaiah 64:6). On our best day it is the blood of Jesus that redeems us. On our worst day it is the blood of Jesus that saves us! We having nothing to boast in of ourselves. Our soul must make its boast in the Lord! Let him that glories, glory in the Lord! We have no rights to judge, condemn and tear down others with our criticisms—not when we would be lost were it not for His amazing grace! Let us love radically and live graciously.

Freely you received it. Now freely give!

And as ye go, preach, saying, The kingdom of heaven
is at hand. Heal the sick, cleanse the lepers, raise the

dead, cast out devils: freely ye have received, freely give (Matthew 10:7-8).

ABOUT THE AUTHOR

James A. McMenis is the senior pastor of Word of God Ministries. He founded the ministry as a weekly Bible study at the age of 22. Through the local assembly, television broadcasts, and conferences, he has dedicated his life to "Preaching Jesus as the Manifested Word of God!" He is known for teaching God's Word in a powerful, fresh, and revelatory manner that always leads to Jesus. Through his sincere, engaging and humorous delivery, he captures a very diverse audience. Pastor James resides in Louisiana with his wife and four children.

Follow Pastor James on Twitter @james_mcmenis.

For more information or resources by Pastor James, visit wogm.com.

CPSIA information can be obtained
at www.ICGtesting.com
Printed in the USA
LVHW081934130422
715898LV00023B/430